the WESTERN WRITERS *of* AMERICA COOKBOOK

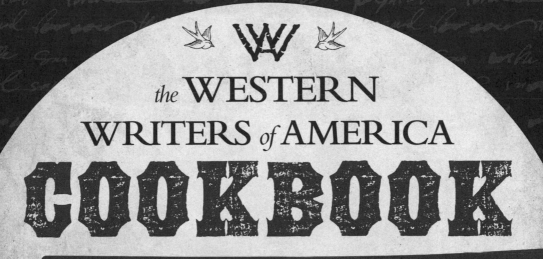

the WESTERN
WRITERS of AMERICA
COOKBOOK

FAVORITE RECIPES, COOKING TIPS, AND WRITING WISDOM

edited by Sherry Monahan, WWA President 2014–2016
& Nancy Plain, WWA Vice President 2016–2018

TWODOT
Guilford, Connecticut
Helena Montana

A · TWODOT® · BOOK

An imprint and registered trademark of Globe Pequot

W is a registered trademark of Western Writers of America

Distributed by NATIONAL BOOK NETWORK

British Library Cataloguing in Publication Information Available
Library of Congress Cataloging-in-Publication Data

ISBN 978-1-4930-2494-0 (paperback)
ISBN 978-1-4930-2495-7 (e-book)

∞™ The paper used in this publication meets the minimum requirements of American National Standard for Information Sciences—Permanence of Paper for Printed Library Materials, ANSI/NISO Z39.48-1992.
Printed in the United States of America

CONTENTS

PREFACE

Western Writers of America, Inc., (WWA) was founded in 1953 to promote the literature of the American West and bestow Spur Awards for distinguished writing in the Western field. The founders were largely authors who wrote traditional Western fiction, but the organization swiftly expanded to include historians, nonfiction authors, young adult and romance writers, and writers interested in regional history.

Literature of the West for the World® describes the collective works of WWA members whose Western literature and includes traditional and contemporary Western fiction, historical analysis, mysteries, biographies, romance, short stories, screen and documentary writing, poems, songs, and more. Our members seek to uncover new facts, deal with new issues, seek more understanding, and offer more for readers to enjoy.

Since its inception, WWA has become the premier Western writer's organization in America and currently boasts over six hundred members. Our members hail from all over the United States as well as other countries across the globe. What unites us is our passion for the American West. No matter where WWA writers physically sit creating our work, the West is always on our minds—and sometimes out our window.

Writers' lives can be solitary, even if we're married and have a family. We do, however, have a chance to share our joys, frustrations, and sorrows once a year with each other. WWA members come together at our annual convention, which ends up being like a family reunion. While we don't have a "dish" to pass at our reunion, we do like to eat.

The editors would like to thank the WWA members who took the time to share their stories, recipes, and photos with us for this fun and tasty project. This book includes recipes from our members, their spouses, publishers, and others who are connected to our organization. We've included some of our favorite dishes to make, eat, or drown our rejection letter sorrows in. You'll find some funny stories, writing tips, snippets of Western history, and much more from our members.

The money earned from this book will go to support our Homestead Foundation. Western Writers of America formed the Homestead Foundation to support its educational and award-giving functions. One way we do this is with our James Ersfeld Memorial Writing Symposiums.

WWA members believe in perpetuating the stories and legends—both past and present—of the American West. The *New York Times* has called Westerns "America's Epic," a part of our culture. We want to ensure the sacrifices and struggles that have built this epic will be remembered by Americans young and old, into the twenty-first century and beyond. We intend to spread the word through our own writing and by inspiring others to read and write stories that are set in the American West.

We do this by granting awards for the best in Western writing; by presenting panels and encouraging the presentation of Western topics at local exhibitions and organizations; and by sponsoring literacy efforts, and encouraging people to read and write about stories set in the American West.

Join us through this culinary journey from those who love to write stories about anything, so long as they are set in the American West. As we sometimes say out West, "Strap on the feedbag!"

Chapter One

Cowboy Up!
(Breakfasts and Quick Breads)

Nothing gets a bleary-eyed author up and out of bed faster than the scent of a freshly brewed cup of coffee or tea. Throw in some sizzling bacon, fluffy hotcakes, and some warm sorghum and we're there! Some of us choose to be healthy and eat fruit or whip up a protein smoothie, too. We all start our days differently. Some of us get dressed as if we're going to an office, and some of us just sit in our "comfy" clothes.

Barbara Dan's Pumpkin Applesauce Muffins

MAKES 24 MEDIUM-SIZE MUFFINS

These muffins have long been a favorite recipe of mine. When my father-in-law lived with our family, he and the children occasionally had a sore throat and had trouble swallowing. Fortunately, these soft, nutritious muffins were regarded as a treat by everyone. (They are just as delicious when eaten by healthy individuals!)

⅔ cup solid vegetable shortening
2⅔ cups sugar
4 eggs
1 cup applesauce
1 cup canned pumpkin
⅔ cup apple juice
3⅓ cups all-purpose flour
2 teaspoons baking soda
½ teaspoon baking powder
1½ teaspoons salt
1 teaspoon cinnamon
½ teaspoon mace
½ teaspoon nutmeg
1 cup walnuts, finely chopped

Preheat the oven to 350°F. Grease the cups of two 12-cup muffin tins or line them with baking cups.

Cream together the shortening and sugar. Add the eggs, one at a time, then stir in the applesauce and pumpkin until well mixed. Add the apple juice, flour, baking soda, and baking powder. Do not overmix.

When the batter is just smooth, add the salt, cinnamon, mace, and nutmeg. Stir in the walnuts. Fill the muffin cups.

Bake for 20 minutes, or until a toothpick inserted in the center of a muffin comes out clean.

Above all, remember that a writer needs a sense of humor.

When baking, never pack down flour in a measuring cup unless specifically told to do so in the recipe.

Barbara Dan's Zucchini Bread

MAKES 1 LOAF

This recipe was born out of dire necessity. Anyone who plants a summer garden will sympathize. One hot summer my son and I planted a modest three hills of zucchini seeds, only to have the vines spread like wildfire and take over the entire garden. The zucchini were enormous—some of them the size of a muscular man's thigh. I am not exaggerating when I say that we couldn't give it away fast enough. We gave it to neighbors, food banks, friends at church, and fellow employees at work. Complicating the harvesting of these prolific vines were a dozen slithery garter snakes who had taken shelter from the sun beneath their heavy foliage! Somehow we weathered the storm. We baked and gave away dozens of loaves of zucchini bread and froze the rest for winter consumption.

PS: I should add that we still plant zucchini every summer and enjoy it wrapped in foil and grilled with other fresh vegetables, or baked as delicious loaves. It's the perfect summer vegetable, no matter how you make it.

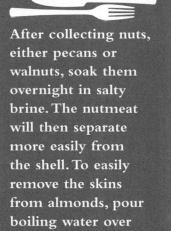

After collecting nuts, either pecans or walnuts, soak them overnight in salty brine. The nutmeat will then separate more easily from the shell. To easily remove the skins from almonds, pour boiling water over them and let them stand for 10 minutes.

Preheat the oven to 350°F.

Beat the eggs until they are fluffy. Add the sugar, oil, and vanilla. Blend well. Stir in the zucchini. Add the sifted dry ingredients and blend into the batter. Fold in the pecans (or nuts of your choice) and pineapple.

Bake in a greased pan for 1 hour or until done.

3 eggs
2 cups sugar
1 cup oil
2 teaspoons vanilla extract
2 cups unpeeled, grated zucchini, packed tight
3 cups flour
1 teaspoon salt
2 teaspoons baking soda
¼ teaspoon baking powder
3 teaspoons cinnamon
½ cup pecans, chopped
1 cup pineapple, drained and crushed

Sherry Monahan's Bear Sign (Doughnuts)

MAKES ABOUT 8 DOUGHNUTS

While doing research for my *Cowboy's Cookbook*, I came across a story of a Wyoming cowboy name Andy Adams. This is Andy's recollection of bear sign on the range: "After dinner our man threw off his overshirt, unbuttoned his red undershirt and turned it in until you could see the hair on his breast. Rolling up his sleeves, he flew at his job once more. He was getting his work reduced to a science by this time. He rolled his dough, cut his dough, and turned out the fine brown bear sign to the satisfaction of all." I found this recipe in a Western newspaper from 1878 that's probably very similar to the doughnuts eaten by Andy and his ranch hands.

1¾ cups flour, sifted

½ teaspoon salt

2 teaspoons baking powder

½ teaspoon baking soda

¾ cup sugar

1 egg, beaten

½ cup buttermilk

1 tablespoon butter, melted

4 cups vegetable shortening or lard for frying

Sift the dry ingredients into a large bowl.

In a separate bowl, beat the egg and sugar until blended. Add the buttermilk to the egg and sugar, followed by the melted butter, and then combine with the dry ingredients. As you mix, the dough should become firm enough to roll. Do not overmix the dough or it will become tough.

Lightly dust the rolling surface with flour and roll out part of the dough into about ¼ inch thick. Cut with a doughnut cutter or shape into doughnuts by hand.

Heat the oil in a deep pot. The oil should be between 350 and 375°F.

Gently drop the doughnuts into the fat and allow to rise, flip, and cook for about 1 or 2 minutes longer. Remove to paper towels and allow to cool.

Frost with your favorite topping or icing or dip into powdered sugar or cinnamon sugar.

Icing

MAKES ENOUGH TO COVER ABOUT 8 DOUGHNUTS

⅓ cup hot water

1 cup confectioners' sugar

Combine the water and sugar in a bowl. Dip the doughnuts while the icing is still warm.

Sandra Dallas's Blueberry Coffee Cake

SERVES 12

I am not much of a cook. Once when an editor was visiting, I baked a cake and was so nervous that I grabbed a can of cornstarch instead of baking powder. What a flop. And one Thanksgiving, I roasted the turkey back-side up and forgot to add the evaporated milk to the pumpkin pie. This blueberry coffee cake, however, has been reliable for fifty years. It's best served the day it's made.

Mix the dry ingredients, then using your fingers or a pastry cutter, cut in the butter until the mixture resembles crumbs. Set aside.

Preheat the oven to 375°F. Butter a 9 x 12-inch pan.

Combine the flour, baking powder, and salt, and set aside.

Cream the butter, then add the sugar. Beat in the egg, then add the vanilla and mix until the batter is fluffy and light.

Add the dry ingredients, milk, and lemon rind, and stir until the ingredients are just combined. Add the blueberries and mix gently.

Spoon the batter into the prepared pan. Sprinkle the top with the chopped pecans and streusel topping. Bake for 50 to 60 minutes.

For the streusel topping:
⅓ cup flour
½ cup sugar
1 teaspoon cinnamon
¼ cup cold butter

For the coffee cake:
2 cups flour
2 teaspoons baking powder
¼ teaspoon salt
¼ cup butter
¾ cup sugar
1 egg
1 teaspoon vanilla extract
½ cup milk
Rind of 1 lemon, grated
2 cups blueberries, washed
    and dried
½ cup pecans, chopped

Just do it! And read Anne Lamott's
Bird by Bird.

Clay Reynolds's Tex-Mex Breakfast

SERVES 4–6

This can be cooked and served any time of the day or night, whenever appetite and a desire for something hearty and hot overcomes the desire to "eat right," or to avoid anything that's not low calorie, low fat, low carb, low taste, gluten free, and void of originality. This is just plain good. And actually, it's pretty healthy, as stuff that's bad for you goes. And it feeds a bunch.

2 tablespoons butter
1 Texas 1015, Bermuda Red, or other onion, coarsely chopped
2 stalks celery, coarsely chopped
½ medium-size bell pepper, coarsely chopped
¼ cup green chiles, finely chopped
¼ cup black olives, sliced
1 clove garlic, minced
4 large fresh tomatoes, blanched and skinned, or 1 (16-ounce) can stewed tomatoes, drained well
Dash of Worcestershire sauce, but only a dash

To check an egg's freshness, put it in a bowl of water. If it floats, throw it away.

Preheat the skillet and melt the butter or margarine, coating the bottom and sides.

Sauté all the chopped vegetables in the melted butter until the onions are transparent. Add the tomatoes and Worcestershire sauce and stir occasionally until the vegetables are fully blended and the whole thing is steaming hot, actually bubbling a bit. Don't worry about any extra liquid forming from the tomatoes. You'll need it.

Using a spatula, form small wells to hold the eggs in the bubbling vegetables at even intervals around the sides of the skillet. Crack the eggs into the wells one at a time, being careful not to break the yolks. Try to make sure that the eggs are well away from the sides of the skillet and are nestled into the small vegetable wells. Salt and pepper the yolks. A drop of Red or Green pepper sauce on each yolk is a nice touch.

Reduce the heat to the lowest setting or lowest flame and cover the skillet. Cook for about 4 minutes, or until the eggs are about three-quarters poached. If necessary, use the spatula to gently separate the vegetables, allowing any uncooked portions of the egg whites to penetrate the entire concoction.

When the eggs are nearly set, add the shredded cheese, sprinkling it generously over the whole thing, being sure to cover the eggs especially well. Cover the skillet and leave the heat on warm until the cheese is completely melted.

Cut the Tex-Mex Breakfast into quarters and serve it with a spatula, directly from the skillet. A steaming pile of fresh tamales goes well with it, as does a spicy salsa, which can be spooned over the top to taste.

This dish can also be served with heated corn tortillas, butter, and the preserves of your choice.

Editing and proofreading are crucial to good writing. It's tough to edit your own work, but try reading it out loud, let it sit for a day or day and then go back.

4–6 eggs, room temperature

Healthy dash of salt

Healthy sprinkle of black pepper

Drop of Red or Green hot sauce

1 cup sharp cheddar cheese, shredded fine

1 9-inch or 12-inch cast-iron skillet (This is the most important item on the list. It must be cast iron, not aluminum, steel, glass, or any sort of nonstick, bright and shiny "chef's pan.")

Krista Soukup's Mother's Chocolate Chip Banana Muffins

MAKES 12 MUFFINS

My four kids love waking up Saturday morning to the smell our family's favorite muffin. This is my mom's recipe that she made for me and my sisters when we were growing up, and now I make for my own kids. My mom, DiAnne, is an exceptional cook and baker who grew up in Minnesota. Her favorite place to travel is "out West," which began as a child with her own father's love of the West.

1½ cups flour
½ cup sugar
2 teaspoons baking powder
½ teaspoon salt
1 egg
½ cup milk
¼ cup vegetable oil
½ cup chocolate chips
¾ cup bananas, mashed
½ cup pecans or walnuts, chopped (optional)

Preheat the oven to 400°F.

Combine all the ingredients in the order given. Stir until blended well.

Pour the batter into muffin cups or greased muffin tins. Bake for 20 to 25 minutes.

Allow to cool slightly and remove from pan and place on baking rack. Serve them warm and the chocolate is gooey!

Joyce Lohse's Cowgirl Crumble Coffee Cake

MAKES 2 COFFEE CAKES; FEEDS 12–16

This recipe is modified from one I discovered during the 1970s. I've used it for years for company, and it never lets me down. It is also great for camping, or events that involve eating outdoors, or combining last-minute ingredients from the chuckwagon.

Preheat the oven to 350°F.

Mix the flour, brown sugar, salt, and shortening till crumbly; reserve ½ cup. To the remaining crumbs, add the baking powder, baking soda, cinnamon, and nutmeg; mix well. Add the buttermilk and eggs; mix well.

Pour into two greased and floured 8-inch baking dishes and top with reserved crumbs. Bake for 25 to 30 minutes. Serve warm.

2½ cups white whole-wheat flour

2 cups brown sugar

½ teaspoon salt

⅔ cup shortening

2 teaspoons baking powder

½ teaspoon baking soda

½ teaspoon ground cinnamon

½ teaspoon ground nutmeg

1 cup buttermilk

2 eggs, beaten (or egg substitute)

Need buttermilk for a recipe? Add 1 teaspoon of white vinegar to 1 cup of milk and let sit for 5 minutes. Voila!

Ann Noble's Pumpkin Chocolate Chip Muffins

MAKES 12 REGULAR-SIZE MUFFINS

This is a favorite at the Chambers House Bed and Breakfast in Pinedale, Wyoming, where breakfast is served in a dining room that originally was the town's first schoolhouse. In addition to being an author, I'm also the owner of the B&B. Muffins are typically considered breakfast food, but these are good snacks all day long. Double the batch, and make plenty. The muffins freeze well in freezer bags.

½ cup (1 stick) butter, melted
1⅔ cups all-purpose flour
1 cup granulated sugar
1 tablespoon pumpkin pie spice
1 teaspoon baking soda
¼ teaspoon baking powder
¼ teaspoon salt
2 large eggs
1 cup plain pumpkin (half of a 1-pound can)
1 cup (6 ounces) chocolate chips

Preheat the oven to 350°F.

Melt the butter, so it has time to cool. Grease the muffin cups or line with baking cups.

In a large bowl, thoroughly mix the flour, sugar, pie spice, baking soda, baking powder, and salt.

In another bowl, break the eggs, then add the pumpkin and melted butter. Whisk until well blended, then stir in the chocolate chips.

Pour the wet mixture over the dry ingredients and fold it in with a rubber spatula just until the dry ingredients are moistened. (This makes for softer muffins.) Scoop the batter evenly into the muffin cups.

Bake 20 to 25 minutes, or until a toothpick comes out clean when pricked into the middle of a muffin. Cool the muffins on a rack, then store them in an airtight container or bag.

Nancy Burgess's Arizona Chilaquiles

SERVES 4

My husband, Jim, and I had a similar dish at a restaurant in Phoenix. We've always been pretty good at figuring out ingredients in recipes, so we experimented and created this recipe. We've been making it for about forty years.

Heat the oil in a large frying pan or electric skillet. Sauté the onions and corn tortillas until the onions are soft. Add the sausage and break it up, cooking until it is no longer pink and then add the green chiles.

Add the eggs and stir constantly, until they are cooked through. Stir the cheese into the mixture just before serving. Cover the pan just long enough for the cheese to melt.

Serve Arizona Chilaquiles with the hot sauce of your choice and slices of avocado.

This dish can be reheated in the microwave on a medium setting.

- 3 tablespoons cooking oil
- 1 medium onion, coarsely chopped
- 8 soft corn tortillas, cut into about 1-inch wedges
- 4–6 ounces bulk pork sausage or chorizo
- 1 (4-ounce) can green chiles, diced, or more to taste
- 8 eggs, lightly beaten
- 2 cups shredded Mexican blend cheese

Candy Moulton's Spudnuts

MAKES ABOUT 3 DOZEN SPUDNUTS

Spudnuts are a form of doughnut. A certain amount of potato is added to change the flavor of the dough and give the fare its unique name. Making and eating spudnuts is a New Year's Day tradition for our family. I usually make at least two or three batches (which is about twelve to fourteen dozen spudnuts), and we invite family and friends. Steve makes the chili and we get the New Year off to a fun (and sweet) beginning. For those of you concerned about calories, I will tell you a secret—there are no calories in spudnut holes!

2 cups milk

⅔ cup shortening

1½ packages fast-rising dry yeast

½ cup warm water

2 eggs, beaten

1 teaspoon salt

½ cup sugar

1 cup potatoes, mashed (Do not use instant potatoes.)

2 teaspoons vanilla extract

6 cups flour

Lard or vegetable oil for frying

To prevent scalded milk from sticking to the saucepan, first rinse the pan with ice-cold water.

Scald the milk and cool it until it is warm. Add the shortening to the warm milk.

In a large bowl, dissolve the yeast in lukewarm water. Beat the eggs slightly, then add them to the warm milk.

Combine the salt and sugar, and add them to the milk mixture. Add this mixture to the yeast mixture in the large bowl.

Add to this the potatoes, vanilla, and 3 cups of flour. Mix well. Add the remaining flour and knead until you have a soft dough. (Add more flour if needed.)

Roll out the dough to ½-inch thickness and cut the spudnuts into a doughnut shape, using a doughnut cutter. Save the holes. Place on lined baking sheets and cover. Let the spudnuts and holes rise in a warm place (beside the woodstove is ideal) for about 1 hour.

Heat the lard or oil to 350°F in a deep fryer or skillet (the oil should be at least 2 inches deep). Fry the spudnuts and holes in the hot lard or oil. As you begin frying, put the uncooked spudnut in the hot grease raised side up; this will allow the unraised bottom of the spudnut to rise, until you turn it one time and let that side cook. Cook each side to a light golden brown, then remove the spudnut from the oil and drain it on a paper towel.

Spudnuts are best glazed. For variety, you can roll the hot spudnuts and holes in sugar, or put sugar in a paper bag, add a few spudnuts and holes, and shake to coat them.

Glaze

Put the teapot on to boil.

Put the powdered sugar in a medium-size bowl, then add the vanilla and enough boiling water (about a cup or so) to make a thin frosting.

Once the glaze is cool enough to handle, dip each spudnut and hole into the glaze, then eat them hot. That's when they are best.

Water
2–3 cups powdered sugar
1 teaspoon vanilla extract

Treat your writing like a job (it is). Go to work every day. Pay yourself, and contribute to your retirement account—faithfully.

Never say no to an assignment. That will keep your plate of projects full. With a full plate of projects, you will not have time for writer's block.

Don't buy anything until you have the money to pay for it. Being debt-free gives you true freedom to write.

G.R. (Honest Doc) Williamson's Dutchman's Date Loaf

MAKES 1 LOAF

This is an updated version of a trail drivers' favorite that cowboys would bribe their trail cook to prepare. There is a tale that one outfit went so far as to promise its cook, known only as "the Dutchman," a night on the town and a bottle of the finest champagne if he would only fix this quick bread in his famous Dutch oven. Well, the cook took them up on their offer, but the cowboys reneged on their promise once they got to Dodge City. The cook then quit the outfit and signed up with a restaurant in town.

1½ cups milk
1 cup oatmeal, uncooked
1 cup dates, chopped
2 cups all-purpose baking mix
⅔ cup sugar
⅓ cup brown sugar
½ cup walnuts, chopped
1 large egg
⅓ cup applesauce
⅓ cup canola oil

Preheat the oven to 325°F.

Place the milk in a 2-cup glass measuring cup and heat it in the microwave until it is almost simmering. Place the oatmeal and dates in a large mixing bowl and stir in the hot milk. After mixing, set this aside to cool to room temperature.

In another bowl, stir together the all-purpose baking mix, sugars, and chopped walnuts. After the oat mixture has cooled, beat in the egg, applesauce, and canola oil. Then stir this mixture into the dry ingredients, mixing well.

Pour the batter into a buttered and floured Bundt or tube pan. Bake for 45 to 50 minutes, or until the top is crusty and golden. Cool the loaf on a rack for 10 minutes before removing it from the pan. Then cool the loaf on the rack for an additional 20 minutes.

Slice and enjoy!

Chapter Two

Ante Up (Appetizers, Soups, and More)

Appetizers, soups, and stews can often sustain an author through deadlines. Sometimes we forget to eat because we're short on time. Eating a quick appetizer or having soup that can serve as a meal for a few days is supper to us.

For those who have calmer lives, try our yummy recipes for appetizers, soups, and stews.

Shanna Hatfield's Cowboy Nachos

SERVES APPROXIMATELY 12

After seeing Cowboy Nachos offered on a restaurant menu, I decided to re-create my own at home. Captain Cavedweller (my husband) seemed appreciative of my efforts as he devoured his second plate of these oh-so-good beefy nachos. You can serve them on small plates as an appetizer or offer a larger serving if you want to make them into a main meal. Since the recipe is so easy to make, it's perfect for a busy day of wrangling words or critters.

2–3 pound beef brisket
1 teaspoon salt
1 tablespoon all-purpose seasoning
1 (14-ounce) can chicken broth
1 (22-ounce) bag waffle fries
2 (14-ounce) cans chili
½ cup sour cream
Barbecue sauce
½ cup shredded cheddar cheese
½ cup sliced black olives

Season the brisket with the salt and seasoning, then place it, along with the chicken broth, in a slow cooker. Cover the pot and cook on medium heat for 8 hours.

About 20 minutes before you are ready to serve the nachos, line a baking tray with the fries and pop them in the oven, following the directions on the package.

While the fries bake, remove the meat from the slow cooker and let it rest for about 5 to 7 minutes. Cut it into thin slices.

Cook the chili according to the directions on the can. (You can microwave the chili since that takes less time, and you can then cook and serve in the same bowl!)

Create an assembly line with the ingredients and allow people to put on their own toppings, or create a huge platter of the nachos. To assemble them, layer the fries, chili, sour cream, meat, barbecue sauce, cheese, and olives.

Hearty, flavorful, and so good!

Micki Fuhrman's Easy Goat Cheese Pesto Dip

SERVES 4–8

I love quick and easy appetizers that I can throw together for a trip to the neighbor's or serve for company to nosh on while I finish cooking dinner. I started making this ridiculously easy two-ingredient dip a few years ago, and it has become a favorite of my friends and family. Sometimes I use olive tapenade or sun-dried tomatoes instead of the pesto, and it's just as tasty. The plastic wrap gives it a finished, elegant look and makes cleanup a snap.

2 tablespoons pesto
1 (8-ounce) goat cheese log, warmed to room temperature
(You will also need plastic wrap and a custard dish or small bowl.)

Line a ½-cup custard-baking dish (or other small microwave-safe bowl) with plastic wrap, leaving some excess at the edges.

Spoon the pesto into the dish, creating a layer at the bottom. Add spoonfuls of the goat cheese to the dish, taking care not to disturb the pesto.

Heat in a microwave at high power for about 15 to 20 seconds. Remove the dish.

Bring the excess plastic wrap up to cover the mixture, gently press down to compact the dip, and then open the plastic wrap again. If you like, you can chill the dip in the refrigerator for a few minutes.

Turn the dish upside down onto a serving platter. Remove the dish, then remove the plastic wrap, and you have a beautiful layered dip. It is excellent with pita chips or table crackers.

I have a family and I'm always involved in multiple projects, so writing every day is not an option. I've started splitting the week into "chore/appointment days" and "writing days" since I work better when I can hyperfocus for hours on one thing.

Linda and Richard Jacobs's Tasty Lamb-Stuffed Grape Leaves

SERVES 4–6

Known variously as dolmas, dolmathes, and other similar names in Greece, Lebanon, and other Middle Eastern destinations, stuffed grape leaves are usually rather dull. They come in cans, oily and stuffed with little but rice. Restaurant versions are better, but usually with little lamb and seasonings and a lot of rice. That's clearly tradition, but Dick and I wanted to make our own version that would work as an entree and be tasty, so here's our recipe.

1 medium onion, diced
2 tablespoons olive oil
1 pound ground lamb
1 cup golden raisins
1 cup currants
1 cup walnut pieces
1 tablespoon sumac
Salt, pepper, and garlic powder, to taste
2 cups precooked rice
1 (8-ounce) jar grape leaves in brine

When using dried fruits like raisins, soak them in a small amount of liquid to rehydrate before cooking with them.

Sauté the onion in olive oil, add the lamb, and cook until the meat is no longer pink. Add the raisins, currants, walnuts, and sumac, and season to taste. Mix in the cooked rice and stir. Let the filling cool enough to be handled comfortably.

Some recipes say to rinse the grape leaves and some say to blanch them. We think that takes away much of the tangy flavor and rich texture.

Grape leaves usually have three lobes. Place the leaf shiny side down on your work surface, and roll up the leaf with about a tablespoon of filling (depends on the size of the leaf). Then fold in the two outer lobes. Start to roll from the stem end of the leaf. Have a pan ready to lay the rolled-up leaves in, so that they don't unroll. The stuffed grape leaves should be roughly ¾ inch in diameter and 1½ to 2 inches long. It really doesn't matter which side of the leaf goes on the outside, but we think the shiny side looks best.

Cover the stuffed grape leaves with foil to prevent drying out, and bake them in a 300°F oven for 20 minutes, until they are heated. Stuffed grape leaves are good hot or cold.

Once, I was interviewed by my publisher, Medallion Press. They asked what I would tell beginning writers. I said, "Do not believe you can rewrite forever, move things around and change them, and fall into the trap of giving up. And self-publish prematurely." Before every one of my six published books went to the publisher, I could read the manuscript out loud without pause. Each sentence flowed into the next, with no choppiness. And I didn't want to change anything! Stay with your editing until you find that place, and your work will be perceived as clean by your publisher, reviewed well by the marketplace, and win multiple awards.

Dorothy's Chicken Wing Appetizer, contributed by Gail L. Jenner

SERVES 4–6

My mother developed this recipe more than fifty years ago and served it frequently at parties and gatherings. She even used orange gelatin in place of lemon, but it's not quite as tasty. The wings are easy to cook, easy to eat (a bit sticky!), and delicious. This is an easy recipe to prepare ahead of time. I often take these to potlucks or serve at family gatherings on holidays. The kids especially love them and come back for seconds. The glass pan and use of nonstick cooking spray makes it a relatively simple cleanup.

16–20 chicken wings
  (I often stock up
  when on sale!)
6 ounces pineapple juice
6 ounces soy sauce
1 (3-ounce) box lemon
  gelatin
2 tablespoons sesame seeds
  (optional)
Salt and pepper, to taste

Preheat the oven to 350°F. Grease or apply cooking spray to a 9 x 13-inch glass baking pan.

Cut the wings into three pieces at the joints. Discard the "tips." Place the wings in the baking dish to cover surface (you can squeeze them together).

In a 2-cup measuring cup or mixing bowl, combine the pineapple juice and soy sauce. Stir and pour over the chicken wings.

Sprinkle the lemon gelatin liberally over the wings and sauce (you may not need to use the entire box, but use at least half). Sprinkle sesame seeds over the wings, if desired.

Bake the wings for 45 minutes or until they are brown and thoroughly cooked.

Season with salt and pepper, if needed. Serve the wings warm or cold.

Use liquid aminos instead of soy sauce. It's much lower in sodium, but still has that amazing flavor.

Jan Cleere's Gold Nuggets

MAKES ABOUT 5½ DOZEN NUGGETS

When I was a child, my father used to make these crispy gold nuggets every Christmas, and I have now added them to my family's holiday celebrations. However, if I need a respite from a long day of research or writing, I am more than happy to whip up a batch of these cheesy golden crackers, no matter what the time of year. They are addictive!

Mix together the flour, salt, and cayenne pepper, and set aside.

In the large bowl of an electric mixer, cream the butter. Add the cheese and beat until thoroughly blended. On low speed, gradually add the dry ingredients, scraping the bowl until the ingredients are thoroughly incorporated.

Spread some flour lightly on a board and turn the dough onto the floured surface. Lightly flour your hands and form the dough into a round shape about 8 inches long and 1½ to 2 inches in diameter.

Wrap the dough in plastic wrap or waxed paper and refrigerate it for several hours or several days. Don't freeze the dough.

Before baking the nuggets, toast the sesame seeds by spreading them in a shallow pan and placing the pan in the middle of an oven preheated to 350°F. Shake the pan occasionally until the seeds turn golden brown, about 15 to 20 minutes. Set the seeds aside to cool.

With a very sharp knife, cut the nuggets to a ⅛-inch thickness and place them about 2 inches apart on an ungreased cookie sheet. Sprinkle the tops of the nuggets generously with the toasted sesame seeds.

Bake the nuggets at 350°F for 12 to 15 minutes, until lightly browned. They must bake long enough to be very crisp, but overbaking burns the cheese.

1 cup all-purpose flour, plus some flour for rolling out the dough
½ teaspoon salt
⅛–½ teaspoon cayenne pepper★
1 stick (¼ pound) butter
½ pound extra sharp cheddar cheese, finely grated
3 tablespoons sesame seeds (optional)

★ For sharp and spicy nuggets, use ½ teaspoon cayenne. With ⅛ teaspoon, they will have a good mild flavor, while ¼ teaspoon will make them warm.

When the nuggets come out of the oven, immediately remove them from the cookie sheets and place them on cooling racks.

Store the nuggets in an airtight container.

Years ago, I took a class from Bob Early, who was editor of Arizona Highways *magazine for many years. He told me to keep a small notebook within reach, as you never know when inspiration will strike. Even today with all our smartphones and tablets, I still carry a notebook with me at all times.*

Cheewa James's Cranberry Brie

SERVES 6–8

In addition to being a Western author, I'm a tennis player and admire the great player Maria Sharapova. She once said, "It's easy to impress me. I don't need a fancy party to be happy. Just good friends, good food, and good laughs. I'm happy. I'm satisfied. I'm content."

My friends are my treasures—the gift I give myself. I bring them together often in my home, at times introducing an interesting new face with a great spirit and a good mind. My friends habitually call these get-togethers "Brie gatherings," named for the appetizer I often serve.

Trim the rind from the top of the Brie, leaving a ½-inch border. Place the Brie on a microwave-safe plate.

Combine the cranberries, pecans, and sugar, and sprinkle the mixture over the Brie. Drizzle it with honey. Cover and chill until it is ready to heat.

Microwave the Brie for 1 to 2 minutes, or just until the cheese is softened. Watch it carefully. Serve with crackers and pear slices.

Tip: For entertaining: If you can't find a 2-pound wheel of Brie, buy four 8-ounce rounds. Divide the topping evenly among the four rounds and microwave them, two at a time, for 1 to 2 minutes or until the Brie softens.

1 8-inch round Brie cheese (about 2 pounds)
¾ cup dried cranberries or sweetened dried cranberries
¾ cup pecans, finely chopped
3 tablespoons light brown sugar
¼ cup honey

Write concise sentences, compact paragraphs, short and understandable words—easy to skim and scan. Get to the point and command attention.

Cheewa James's Curry Dip

SERVES 6–8

At Christmastime a few years ago, I stumbled on a wonderful idea for my sons' gifts. Both grown and with families of their own, whenever the boys—excuse me, they are now referred to as men—are invited to dinner in my home, they always remind me of favorite dishes I made for them in their youth: Spanish rice, Cherokee casserole, curry dip, lemon cake (today made with lemons from my own trees), and other Cheewa specialties. So for Christmas, I made David and Todd each a recipe book of these cherished dishes with the recipe cards handwritten (that was the hardest part).

1 cup mayonnaise
2 teaspoons curry powder
1 tablespoon Worcestershire
   sauce
3 tablespoons ketchup
½ teaspoon garlic salt

Combine all the ingredients in a bowl. Chill and serve as a dip with raw cauliflower, celery, and green peppers.

Be a storyteller: Readers will more easily retain the story, bringing the point of the whole thing into focus and stamped on the brain.

Susan Cummins Miller's Salmon Cheese Ball

SERVES 6

My father, who was born at a coal mine in Montana a century ago, never fully adapted to city life. On weekends and long holidays, we'd escape from Pasadena to camp in the desert, on Southern California or Baja beaches, or on the shores of western lakes or rivers. In the Sierra Nevada and at Sandpoint, Idaho, we trawled for kokanee, a landlocked salmon. When my parents retired, they canned much of their catch for winter use—and shared the bounty. Kokanee and commercially canned salmon work equally well in this holiday recipe I adapted from one my mother made.

Chop the parsley leaves and set them aside.

Combine all the ingredients, except the parsley, with the cream cheese in a bowl.

Shape the mixture into a ball and roll it in the parsley until covered. Wrap the ball in plastic wrap and chill it for at least 1 hour.

To serve, spread the cheese on crackers or fresh vegetables.

1 bunch Italian flat parsley, washed and patted dry
1 cup chopped or flaked cooked salmon or kokanee (canned, smoked, etc.)
1 tablespoon onion, freshly grated
1 tablespoon garlic, minced
1 tablespoon dill weed (fresh or dried)
2 or more dashes of Tabasco, Sriracha, or similar chile sauce, to taste
Juice from ½ lemon
8 ounces cream cheese

Susan Cummins Miller's Turkey Tortilla Soup

SERVES 4–6, DEPENDING ON WHETHER USED AS A FIRST COURSE OR AN ENTREE

When I was nine, my family adopted a new Thanksgiving tradition—camping with friends at Morro Bay, California, for the holiday weekend. Each family cooked its turkey in a trailer oven or over a campfire, and we then gathered around tables laden with food. My mother roasted the largest bird she could find, which guaranteed plenty of leftovers. I follow in her footsteps.

A friend from those old Morro Bay days introduced me to chicken tortilla soup when I moved to Tucson. I played with the recipe, substituting leftover turkey broth and meat for chicken. The resulting soup is rich and satisfying.

8 corn tortillas, cut into thin strips★
1 tablespoon olive oil
3 cloves garlic, minced
4 green onions, chopped
1 large Anaheim chile (or mild jalapeño), minced
3 cups cooked turkey, cut into bite-size pieces
8 cups turkey or chicken stock
¼ cup cilantro, chopped
1 ripe avocado, diced
1 cup Monterey Jack or 4-cheese mix, grated

★Two cups of broken corn tortilla chips may be substituted for the browned corn tortilla strips. If so, skip the first step in the recipe.

Heat the oven to 350°F. Spread the tortilla strips on a cookie sheet and bake until they are lightly browned. Set them aside.

In a large soup pot, heat the olive oil over medium heat and sauté the garlic, onions, and chile for 4 to 5 minutes.

Add the turkey, turkey stock, and cilantro. Bring the soup to a boil, and simmer for 15 minutes.

Add the avocado and cheese, return the soup to a boil, and then remove it from the heat. Cover and let stand for 5 minutes.

Top the individual servings with browned tortilla strips.

Trish Schmelzer's Polar Vortex Bean Soup, contributed by Paul Colt

SERVES 6

Come wintertime it can get downright cold on the eastern porch to the Great Plains. One of those frozen festivals inspired this recipe from my wife, Trish Schmelzer.

Inspect the dried beans for pebbles, then give them a good rinse. Place the beans in a large kettle and add 2 quarts cold water. Simmer for 2 minutes, remove them from the heat, cover them, and let them stand 1 hour. Do not drain them. Add the pork shank, salt, peppercorns, and bay leaf. Cover the kettle and simmer 3 hours.

Add the onion. Remove the shank. Simmer the soup for 1 hour. Shred the meat from the shank and return the meat to the simmering soup. Adjust salt to taste.

- 1 (20-ounce) bag 16-bean soup mix (Do not use the enclosed seasoning packet.)
- 1 2 lb. bone-in smoked pork shank
- ½ teaspoon kosher salt
- 6 whole peppercorns
- 1 bay leaf
- 1 small onion, diced

The first thing an aspiring writer needs to understand is that writing is a journey. To complete the journey, you need determination and perseverance. You need thick skin to handle rejection. You need the ability to take criticism and use it to get better. If that doesn't sound like you, rent a movie. Writing is a craft you have to learn. You may come to writing thinking you know how, but you don't know the craft. You need somebody to critique your work. I mean really critique your work. Take the criticism and use it to get better. When I coach aspiring writers, the first lesson is nearly always the same: simple sentence, present tense, active voice. If you don't remember those concepts, run, don't walk, to the nearest grammar text and read up. Then practice.

Carol Crigger's Creamy Cauliflower Soup

SERVES 6–8

Except for my grandmother's banana bread "receipt," I've never used a recipe I didn't tweak, even if only a little. This one, like my other submissions, has been tweaked quite a lot. I love making soup, and this one is an old favorite. It's also a good way to use the veggies that have been collecting in your refrigerator while you've been immersed in a crucial scene in your WIP (author lingo for work in progress). Cook fresh! When I make this soup, I always use white cauliflower, but the green or yellow or purple varieties might be intriguing, too. Like bacon? (And who doesn't?) Add some if you like.

2 carrots, diced
1 medium onion, chopped
2 stalks celery (with leaves), chopped
¼ cup green pepper, chopped
2 cups cauliflower, cut in small pieces
1 medium potato, diced
1 cup mushrooms, chopped
⅓ cup butter
4 cups chicken stock
Couple pinches of thyme leaves
2 tablespoons soy sauce
¼ cup flour
2 cups whole milk
Salt and pepper, to taste
1 cup sharp cheddar cheese, grated

Cook the vegetables for 3 minutes in a little olive oil or some of the butter. Add the chicken stock, thyme, and soy sauce, and simmer for 15 minutes or until done. Break up the chunks with a potato masher, but don't make it too smooth.

Place the remaining butter (melted) and flour in a small saucepan. Add the milk and stir until thickened. Add to the soup.

Add the salt and pepper, and stir in the cheese. Serve as soon as the cheese is melted.

Ann McCord's Cheesy Potato Soup, contributed by Monty McCord

SERVES 8 (1 CUP OF SOUP EACH)

My wife Ann's mother taught her how to make simple potato soup—no measuring, just add things until the soup looked right. Since then, Ann has improved on this recipe by adding bacon and cheese. This creamy soup, with a side of crackers and slices of summer sausage, makes a quick and tasty meal on a cold night. How can a man who claims Irish roots not like good potato soup?

Add the potatoes, onion, celery, chicken broth, and pepper to a 4- or 5-quart saucepan. Cover the pan and bring its contents to a boil. Reduce the heat and simmer for 30 minutes, or until the potatoes are very tender.

Whisk together the table cream, milk, and flour. Slowly add this to the soup mixture, stirring constantly to prevent lumps. Simmer for 10 minutes, until the soup thickens to a creamy consistency. Stir in the cheese. Season the soup with the salt and pepper to taste.

Just before serving, garnish the soup with the crumbled bacon and cheesy snack crackers.

4 large potatoes, peeled and cubed (½-inch cubes)
1 cup yellow onion, finely diced
½ cup celery, finely diced
4 cups chicken broth
¼ teaspoon pepper
1 cup table cream★
1 cup 2% milk★
2 tablespoons flour
1½ cups cheese (American or cheddar blend), finely shredded
Salt and pepper, to taste
6–8 strips bacon, cooked crisp and crumbled
Cheesy snack crackers

★Fat-free half-and-half and skim milk may be substituted for the table cream and 2% milk, if desired.

Rocky Gibbons's Easy Clam Chowder

SERVES 6

On Christmas Eve, it was tradition at our house to have clam chowder in bread bowls. This recipe is a variation of one my mother originated. It's easy and delicious!

3 (6.5-ounce) cans chopped clams
2 cups finely diced potatoes
1 cup minced celery
1 cup minced onion
¾ cup butter, melted
¾ cup flour
1 quart half-and-half
½ teaspoon salt
½ teaspoon sugar
Dash of pepper
2 teaspoons red wine vinegar
Small splash of red wine, or to taste

Drain the juice from the clams, pouring it over the potatoes, celery, and onion in a medium saucepan. Add water to barely cover the contents of the pan. Simmer about 20 minutes over medium heat until the potatoes are tender.

In a separate saucepan, add the butter and flour. Cook about 1 to 2 minutes, stirring constantly. Add the half-and-half and cook, stirring until smooth and thick. Add the undrained vegetables and clams. Season to taste with the salt, sugar, pepper, vinegar, and red wine.

Note: If the soup is too thick, thin it with a little cream.

Freshly ground pepper tastes much better than pre-ground.

Dawn Senior-Trask's Chicken Soup

SERVES 8–10

I experimented until I found the combination of ingredients that most reminded me of the chicken soup that my mother, Aileen Senior, made to keep us happy and healthy during my childhood in a log cabin in the mountain foothills near Saratoga, Wyoming. My mom cooked on a wood range for years. This soup is not a low-fat version but is meant to feed people who work hard outdoors in the winter. It satisfies, and now with just my husband and me at home, I don't have to cook again for several days. A great dish to cook when I want a nice stretch of writing time! Speaking of writing, my advice is, toss everything into your first draft! In contrast to cooking, in writing you can always fish stuff out again.

In a large pot, cover the whole chicken(s) with water, add a little salt and pepper, and bring it to a boil. Turn the burner to low and cover. Simmer about 2 hours.

Remove the chicken from the pot and place it on a large platter. Let it cool. Add to the pot the carrots, onion, celery, peas, and parsley.

Remove the chicken meat from the bones, break the meat into small pieces, and return the pieces to the pot. Cook at a low temperature until the vegetables are tender. Add the noodles to the soup and cook the length of time according to the directions for the noodle type. Add the cream. Heat the soup but do not boil.

1 large or 2 small chickens, skinned and trimmed
Water, as needed
Salt and pepper, to taste
2–3 carrots, chopped
½ onion, chopped
2–3 celery ribs, chopped
1 cup frozen peas
1 small bunch fresh or 1 tablespoon dried parsley
½ pound wide noodles
½ pint heavy cream

Rod Miller's Desperation Dinner
Fast and Furious Bean Soup

FEEDS 4, DEPENDING ON AMPLITUDE OF APPETITE

One day after hours of fingering the keyboard, my well-fed middle reminded me that dining was overdue. Near collapse, I raided the refrigerator and staggered into the pantry to see what the racks and shelves might inspire. This simple and easy soup is the result. "Foodies" will likely turn up their noses at such unassuming fare, but low-rent types like me shovel it in with gusto and glee. It's a meal all by itself if you butter some bread or a biscuit for sopping purposes.

1 cup diced, uncooked bacon (I buy a brick of ends and pieces for this sort of thing, but any baconized pork belly will do.)

1 cup diced raw onion

44 ounces canned pinto beans (I use a 29-ounce can and a 15-ounce can, but if you use three of the small cans, I don't suppose the extra ounce of beans would matter.)

1 (4-ounce) can diced green chiles

Cook the bacon in a small skillet, adding the onions once the pan is well lubricated. Stir frequently.

Dump the beans and green chiles into a saucepan or pot of suitable size (my wife says the one I use is 3 quarts) and fire up the stove.

When the bacon is cooked to your liking and the onions are tender, dump the entire contents of the skillet into the beans and stir.

As the contents of the pot bubble, smash some of the beans against the side with a hefty spoon to thicken things up a bit.

That's all. Eat.

Always use fresh ingredients, stir words until blended smoothly, season sparingly, let simmer before serving.

Emil Franzi's Snake Killer's Posole

SERVES 6–8

After submitting this recipe to Western Writers of America, I thought it might make a nice segment on my show, *Voices of the West*. I tossed out these comments for consideration: "OK. Actresses and snake killing. Barbara Stanwyck would've had no problem. Maureen O'Hara would've been quite capable but would prefer to order some man to kill it for her. Take it from there: Who would've then eaten it? Who would've eaten it while still alive? Who would've taken it home for a pet? Who would've faked being afraid? Who really would have been afraid?"

Snake Killer's Posole is always better the next day.

Sauté the onion and garlic in the oil, until they are soft. Add the spices.

Stir in the meat, hominy, broth, tomatoes, and chiles.

Cook the posole covered and on low heat. Simmer for 45 to 60 minutes.

1 onion, chopped
2 cloves garlic, chopped
2 tablespoons olive oil
½ teaspoon pepper
Salt, to taste
½ teaspoon cumin
½ teaspoon cloves
1½ pounds cooked meat (Pork is best, but chicken or anything else is OK.)
1 (29-ounce) can hominy, drained
3–5 cups beef broth
1 (28-ounce) can diced tomatoes
1 (4-ounce) can diced green chiles

Jan C. Hill's Gazpacho (Spanish Cold Soup)

SERVES 6–8

This family recipe was handed down to me by my mother, Dorothy Christelman. It was a favorite that she would often serve with a light supper on warm summer evenings and also at large extended family gatherings. In addition to serving it to my family, I now include it on the menu for our harvest-themed dinner, a gathering of friends held at our home every October. It is also healthful and low-calorie. The recipe has been given to others who have modified it by adding or substituting ingredients such as red peppers, Worcestershire sauce, or more juice, but we prefer it as is.

1 medium cucumber, cut into pieces (about ¾-inch chunks)

1 medium green pepper, seeded and cut into pieces

1 medium Spanish onion, sliced

6 tomatoes, peeled (To peel, place the tomatoes briefly into boiling water, remove to cold water, then peel.)

3 cloves garlic, finely minced

3 tablespoons red wine vinegar

3 tablespoons olive oil

1 tablespoon finely chopped basil

1 teaspoon salt

1 quart tomato juice (Sacramento brand preferred)

Croutons for garnish, if desired

Place the cucumber in a food processor. Using the pulse setting, chop it, but do not emulsify. Empty the contents into a large bowl.

Repeat the process separately with the green pepper, onion, and tomatoes. Place each ingredient into the same large bowl.

Add the garlic, vinegar, olive oil, basil, salt, and tomato juice. Stir well. Chill well until ready to serve.

Garnish the soup with croutons when served, if desired.

Lucia Robson's Mexican Winter Squash Soup

SERVES 8

This Mexican winter squash soup is my go-to recipe for myself and for friends who like food spicy.

Rinse, trim, and peel the squash. Chop it and then boil it in the stock until tender.

In a large, heavy-bottomed 3-quart pot, warm the butter, then add the leeks and salt. Cook until tender. Add the garlic, cumin, and chili powder. Cook for 1 minute.

Add the squash and stock, tomatoes, chipotles, and cilantro bottoms. Cook for 30 minutes.

Puree the soup. Garnish it with the sour cream and cilantro.

1 2-pound butternut squash
6 cups chicken or vegetable stock
1½ tablespoons unsalted butter
2–3 cups chopped leeks (white and light green parts only)
¼ teaspoon salt, or to taste
½ teaspoon minced garlic
½ teaspoon ground cumin
¼ teaspoon chili powder
1 cup crushed tomatoes
1–2 chipotle peppers in adobo, minced and seeds removed
2 cilantro bottoms (stems) with roots, cleaned and minced
8 teaspoons sour cream, for garnish
3 tablespoons chopped cilantro, for garnish

Anne Hillerman's Lazy Writer's Chicken Soup

SERVES 6

What smells better than a pot of chicken soup simmering on the stove? What is a better get-well present than a container of soup that can be eaten right then or saved for when the appetite improves? This recipe, a Santa Fe variation on an American classic, appeals to me because of the spice of the chipotle and the sweetness of the garbanzos. I like to serve it with a dish of lime wedges to squeeze in for extra zest. Be sure to notice the colors—the beautiful light green of the avocado and the red of the tomatoes against the golden broth.

2 whole chicken breasts
10 cups water
½ cup diced onion
½ cup diced celery
1 tablespoon salt
2 bay leaves
2 (10- or 12-ounce) cans
 garbanzo beans
2 large, ripe, fresh tomatoes,
 diced
¼ cup fresh cilantro,
 chopped
1 (7-ounce) can chipotle
 peppers in adobo sauce,
 drained
Salt and pepper, to taste
2 soft avocados, diced

Cook the chicken breasts in a stockpot with the water, onion, celery, salt, and bay leaves. Remove the bay leaves and discard them. Remove the chicken and cool. Reserve the stock and set aside.

Remove the bones and skin from the chicken, dice the meat, and return it to the stock.

Drain the garbanzo beans and add them along with the tomatoes, cilantro, and chipotle peppers. Salt and pepper to taste.

Bring to a boil, then simmer for about 15 minutes on low heat. Garnish with diced avocado and serve the soup hot.

Note: You can also make this soup as a quicker meal with prepared chicken stock and precooked breast meat. Or use your own homemade stock recipe and add the vegetables.

Sandy Whiting's Bean Soup That Sam Elliott Would Also Love!

SERVES 4–8

While scarfing this down, think of Sam Elliott's character in the movie *Conagher*. I don't care for beans, but his character convinced me to try this soup. Turned out, he was right! Beans are good!

Soak the beans overnight in cold water. Drain and rinse them.

In a large stockpot or Dutch oven, add 8 cups warm water. Add the beans, ham bone, carrot, black pepper, basil, tomatoes, and brown sugar.

Simmer on low heat (or over hot campfire coals) for a couple hours or so. The soup is done when the beans are soft.

½ pound dry white beans
1 very meaty ham bone
1 large carrot, shredded
¼ teaspoon black pepper
Pinch of basil
1 (16-ounce) can diced tomatoes, or 2 cups fresh tomatoes, chopped
1 tablespoon brown sugar

Gail L. Jenner's Minestrone Soup

SERVES 4–6

As cattle ranchers, we find ways to use all cuts of beef. Soup in winter is hearty and an "easy fix." I love shanks for their flavor and texture; they make rich and nutritious broth (because of the bones) and are relatively inexpensive. I serve this frequently, and it's a soup that can be expanded. It's also a good way to include varieties of vegetables (turnips or parsnips, too). I use dry beans or lentils if I have the time to let them cook. It's easy to prepare in a slow cooker when I am working away from the house.

2 beef shanks (Jenner Family Beef shanks are perfect!)
2 quarts water
Salt and pepper
1 (15-ounce) can beans (white, navy, or red)
½ cup rice (brown or white)
1 whole onion, chopped
2–3 carrots, chopped
½ cup chopped celery
3 potatoes, chopped
½ cup chopped garlic
1 (16-ounce) can diced tomatoes
1½ teaspoons dried basil
½ teaspoon dried oregano
Pinch of red pepper flakes (optional)
½ cup chopped spinach or kale

Early in the day, or the day before, put into a large soup pot the beef shanks, water, 1 teaspoon salt, and 1 teaspoon pepper. Bring this to a boil, then cover the pot and lower the temperature to medium heat. Cook the beef shanks until tender, about 2 hours.

Cool. Remove the bones and skim the fat. Return the meat to the liquid.

Add to the beef and beef broth the beans, rice, onion, carrots, celery, potatoes, garlic, and salt and pepper to taste. Cook this for another hour, or longer. If it is too thick, add more water.

Add the tomatoes, basil, oregano, red pepper flakes, spinach or kale, and additional salt and pepper as needed. Cook for 20 minutes, or until the soup is boiling hot.

Serve the minestrone with freshly grated Parmesan cheese and crusty French bread.

Keep *writing: It's the writers who finish who publish! Ask for and accept criticism. It's hard to suffer through in the beginning, but it's imperative. Writing really is about "rewriting"! Attend conferences, join a critique group, even enter contests: These things will help you "get out of your own way" and you can network, learn, and gain opportunities to pitch or meet other authors.*

Stephen Bly's Buffalo Soup

I fixed this soup for a church potluck a time or two. I found out who the hardy ones in the bunch were—mainly the hunters. Personally, I believe rattlesnake bar-b-qued and cut up into tasty tidbits is good. Some miss out on culinary delights because of the narrowness of their menu. Now, you say, where do you get bison meat? From my buddy up in Weippe, Idaho, who raises them. Many stores across America carry bison as well.

2–3 pounds bison meat (Nope, they are not an endangered species.)

2 tablespoons (more or less) vegetable oil

5 pieces bacon (No, you may not use artificial bacon bits.)

2 (16-ounce) packages mixed veggies

½ tad of garlic powder

2 tads black pepper, ground

A tad (more or less) of paprika

2 tablespoons granulated sugar

1 package dry onion soup mix

1 (16-ounce) can tomato sauce (Don't buy the cheap brand.)

1 (15-ounce) jar chunky medium salsa (Hot, if you dare.)

4 (14- or 15-ounce) cans beef broth

Your trusty big container of Montreal Steak Seasoning

It goes without saying: red pepper sauce

Brown the bison in the oil and set aside.

Fry your bacon crisp, then sponge off the excess oil with paper towels and crumble (that means grab it in your hand and maul it like a two-year-old).

Get out your really big kettle and toss in the veggies (even frozen ones work here), garlic powder, black pepper, paprika (it's that red-looking stuff that is normally only used on deviled eggs at church potlucks), sugar, onion soup mix, tomato sauce, chunky salsa, mauled bacon, and the browned buffalo meat. Then add 4 cans of beef broth. As you stir it all together, sprinkle generous portions of steak seasoning.

Now, sit that on the big burner and toss in another chunk of wood, 'cause you want to bring it up to a boil (or turn the burner up to high). Then, reduce the heat to low and partially cover the kettle. Let it simmer until the neighbor finishes showing you their digital vacation pics. (Usually a couple of hours is nice.)

All the while, you can take a sip or two to determine just how much Tabasco you need to add to bring out the "boisterous" in it. By itself, it goes well with homemade sourdough bread and a green salad with jalapeños.

Here are some of my writing tips:
1.) Stand in front of a full-length
mirror and read your manuscript aloud.
If you get distracted by what you look
like, the chapter is too boring.
2.) If the plot drags, shoot someone!

Kellen Cutsforth's Mom's Taco Soup

SERVES 4–6

This recipe was created by my mom, Patricia Cutsforth, during the Christmas season as a meal for her grown-up children to enjoy as they arrived home for the holidays. This soup is great for cold and snowy nights or can serve as a nice hot breakfast on a chilly winter morning. A good complement to any meal, the dish is also hardy enough to stand alone as a main course. The soup's Southwestern flavors and ingredients are symbolic of the part of the country where it was first created, on Colorado's southeastern plains near the historic Santa Fe Trail.

1½ pounds ground beef

1 small onion, diced

1 (15-ounce) can hominy, drained

1 (15-ounce) can pinto beans

1 (15-ounce) can kidney beans

3 (14.5-ounce) cans whole tomatoes

1 (4-ounce) can diced green chiles

1 package taco seasoning mix

1 package ranch dressing mix

Optional toppings: grated cheese, sour cream, cilantro, pico de gallo, diced onions

Place a large stock pot or Dutch oven over medium heat. Brown the beef and onion until the beef is no longer pink and the onion is soft. Drain. Add the remaining ingredients and stir them together. Simmer 30 minutes or longer.

If desired, add the toppings to the soup and serve it with tortilla chips, cornbread muffins, or tortillas.

Johnny D. Boggs's Pork Posole

SERVES 8–10

I grew up on grits. But Rodney Ammons, a leather artisan known for his awesome cowboy boots, introduced me to posole at a restaurant in Santa Fe shortly after I moved to New Mexico from Dallas, Texas. Since then, it has been one of my lifelong quests to find the best posole in America. So far, my neighbor remains tops. I'm a distant second. A traditional Mexican dish (soup or stew) made from hominy, posole dates as early as 1500. My native New Mexican neighbor gave me a few tips, though she refused to give me her recipe. I don't take it personally. Her daughter says her mother won't give her the recipe either. Besides, Betty Jean often brings over plenty of posole to our house on Christmas.

Season the pork cubes with garlic salt and pepper, then brown them in the oven.

Fry the bacon in a pan. Remove the bacon when done, but keep the grease in the pan.

Put the posole (do not use cans of hominy!) in a large pot and cover it with water. Add the garlic cloves, bring the water to a boil, and cook until the posole is popping. Drain the posole. Do not reuse this water.

Rinse the pot and return the posole and garlic to it (or use a new pot). Cover the posole with the chicken broth and add the olive oil. Cook over low to medium heat and do not overboil. Thin the posole with water or Mexican beer as needed.

Chop the bacon and dump it into the pot, along with the bacon grease from the frying pan. Add the browned pork meat, diced onions, chopped green chiles, and chopped tomatoes. Add the red chili powder, oregano, and chopped cilantro.

Simmer uncovered for about 1 hour (or until done), stirring as needed. Add salt and pepper to taste. Add more water or beer if needed.

Garnish the posole with the fresh cilantro leaves and serve it with lime wedges and warm tortillas.

2 pounds cubed pork
Garlic salt
Black pepper
4 slices bacon
1 (32-ounce) package posole (Bueno preferred)
6 cloves garlic
4 cups chicken broth
2 tablespoons olive oil
1 bottle dark Mexican beer, as needed
2 large onions, diced
12 green chiles, chopped
3 tomatoes, chopped
2 tablespoons red chili powder
2 tablespoons fresh Mexican oregano, chopped
2 tablespoons cilantro, chopped
Salt and pepper, to taste
Fresh cilantro leaves, for garnish
Lime wedges, for garnish

Bill Groneman's Mama DeLaurenzo's Tubetti Soup (aka Gram's Special Soup)

NUMBER SERVED: VARIABLE—BUT DOUBLE THE NUMBER FOR OTIS (OTHER THAN ITALIANS)

This is an ancient ancestral recipe my mother brought over from the old country (Brooklyn). It can be served before a main course or stand as a meal in itself. It is best served on chilly New York City winter days. It is better still when there are a bunch of Italian relatives laughing and talking at the top of their lungs around the table. Madonna! It'sa good!! Recipe created by Jean Novak (Bill Groneman's mom).

4–5 small marrow bones
1 London broil (about 1–1½ pounds)
1 1-lb. bag whole carrots
1 head celery
1 (8-ounce) can tomato sauce
5 beef bouillon cubes
1 (16-ounce) box pasta, ditalini or tubetti

Put the marrow bones and the meat in a 5-quart pot and fill it with water. Cook on a low flame (do not boil) for 2 hours. Skim the top a few times while it is cooking.

Slice the carrots into penny-size pieces. (Yes, you read it correctly—penny-size.) Cut up the celery.

After 2 hours, remove the bones (from the pot, not your own) and discard them. Add the carrots, celery, tomato sauce, and bouillon cubes. Slow cook the soup for 2 more hours.

Cut the London broil in half and leave it in the soup. Refrigerate the soup overnight.

The next day, skim the soup once again. Remove the meat, cut it into small pieces, and return it to the pot. Warm the soup over medium heat.

In a separate pot, cook the pasta, drain it, and add it to the soup.

Serve the soup when it is warm or hot enough. Serve it with a good Italian or semolina bread and butter, along with a wine that is red to burgundy in color, something hearty.

Bill Groneman's Emergency Chicken Soup

NUMBER SERVED: VARIABLE

This is called "Emergency Chicken Soup" for several reasons. It can be used to treat everything from the sniffles to full-blown colds, or general aches and pains. It can also be prepared in an hour with a minimum of preparation. It is easy to make and one can do so while watching Seinfeld reruns on the television. It is excellent on chilly or cold days. When making this soup it is important that it never comes out the same way twice (see variations below). It is best prepared while enjoying a nip of Hiram-Walker Blackberry Brandy and an occasional sip of Amstel Light Beer.

Put 3 or 4 inches of water in a 5-quart pot. Add the bouillon soup mix, and chicken breasts. Add the peas, green beans, broccoli, mushrooms, and carrots in proportions that are good for you. I prefer it to be more "vegetablier." Add the celery. Add a sprinkle of ground black pepper, a dash of the Marsala cooking wine, and a little onion powder.

Once everything is in, crank up the heat a little (medium-high heat) and cover the pot. Keep an eye on it, stirring frequently. Don't let it boil too violently.

Cook the egg noodles in a smaller pot per package instructions.

After the soup has been going for a while, take out the chicken, cut it up into small pieces, and return it to the pot. Drain the noodles and add to soup.

Turn off the heat and let it stand there for a while. Keep stirring occasionally, though. (The usual cooking time is about 1½ hours, but it can be done in an hour, depending on the emergency.)

Boom! Chow's on!

1 chicken bouillon cube
1 pouch dry chicken noodle soup mix
2 boneless chicken breasts
1 (10-ounce) bag frozen peas
1 (10-ounce) bag frozen cut green beans
1 (10-ounce) bag frozen broccoli, florets or chopped
1 (8-ounce) jar sliced mushrooms, or 1½ lb. fresh mushrooms, cleaned and sliced
1 (10-ounce) bag shoestring carrots
2–3 stalks celery, cleaned and thinly sliced
1 diced tomato
1 jar roasted red peppers, to taste
Ground black pepper, to taste
Marsala cooking wine
A little onion powder
1 (12-ounce) bag egg noodles

Audrey Smith's Siete Mares (Soup of the Seven Seas), contributed by Brad Smith

SERVES 8

My wife and I traveled one hot summer to a resort town on the Pacific coast of Mexico. We learned of a nice little seafood restaurant and decided to give it a try. We got on the bus, and it kept going farther and farther out of town. Finally, at the terminus of the bus line, there sat this little restaurant, right on the beach. It overlooked three tiny islands. The restaurant served up a great seafood medley, from which this recipe originates.

This soup is a fiesta in a bowl. It depends largely on what ingredients are available, so feel free to use frozen ingredients, add more or less of any item, or substitute with different seafood.

1 tablespoon olive oil
½ white onion, diced
½ bell pepper, diced
1 pound large shrimp, shelled
1 pound squid, sliced
1 pound mussels
1 pound small clams
1 (6.5-ounce) can whole baby clams, with liquid
1 (6–7-ounce) can crab, picked over
8 cups bottled clam/tomato juice
1–2 teaspoons powdered chipotle (optional)
Cilantro sprigs
Lime wedges
Flour tortillas

In a large stockpot, sauté the onion and bell pepper in the oil until tender.

Add the seafood and clam/tomato juice. Bring the soup to a boil. Cover it and reduce the heat. Simmer 15 minutes, or until the seafood is done.

Adjust the broth with the powdered chipotle, if you like. Serve the soup with cilantro sprigs, lime wedges, and flour tortillas.

Chapter Three

Side Saddle (Breads, Side Dishes, and Vegetables)

Side dishes and bread are like sidebars to authors. They're not always needed, but they often add something that complements the main dish or story.

In this chapter our members have shared some pretty tasty dishes—so tasty that they can be stand-alone main meals!

Maxine Isackson's So Good French Bread

MAKES 2 LOAVES

I take this bread, sliced and buttered, to "carry in" suppers. Never any left to take home!

3 cups warm water
1 package yeast
⅓ cup sugar
¼ cup oil
1 tablespoon salt
6 cups bread flour

Pour the warm water into a large bowl and add the yeast and sugar. Let this stand for a minute, then add the oil and salt. Add the flour slowly and stir until it is smooth.

Put the dough on a floured board and knead it well, until the dough can be handled easily. Then put it in an oiled bowl, cover it, and let it rise to double its bulk.

Cut the risen dough into two portions. Stretch one portion to the desired length. Press or roll it into an oblong shape, about 13 by 8 inches. Then roll it like a jelly roll, starting on the short side. Repeat this with the second portion of dough. Both loaves should fit on one greased cookie sheet.

Cover and let the dough rise again until it is light.

Bake at 350°F, until the bread is golden brown. If you want a crisper bread, leave it in the oven a bit longer. Let it cool before slicing.

Johnny Boggs's Sweet Chile Cornbread

SERVES 8–9

You grow up in the South, and you learn pretty quickly that cornbread can be sent straight from Heaven. You move to New Mexico, and you quickly discover that fresh green chiles are a gift from God. So . . . my South by Southwestern roots meant a quick blend of cultures. I serve cornbread often when I'm making chili—FYI, chili is the stewed dish, chile is the fruit—for a poker group, or when I need a quick, easy-to-fix bread dish to satisfy a sweet tooth with a bit of pick-me-up kick.

Preheat the oven to 425°F.

In any order, put the dry ingredients in a large bowl and mix, then stir in the diced chiles. Add the milk, egg, oil, and honey. Beat about 1 minute, until smooth.

Pour the mixture into a well-greased and lightly floured 8-inch square baking pan. Bake for 20 to 25 minutes, until the cornbread is golden brown on top and a wooden toothpick inserted into the center is clean when removed.

¾ cup all-purpose flour
¼ cup cake flour
1 cup yellow cornmeal
3 tablespoons white sugar
2 tablespoons brown sugar
4 teaspoons baking powder
4 green chiles that have been roasted, peeled, rinsed, and diced
1 cup milk
1 egg
¼ cup canola oil (at high altitude, add 2 tablespoons oil)
2 tablespoons honey

When baking, if a recipe calls for water and something sticky like honey or oil, measure the water first and then the honey or oil. to prevent the honey or oil from sticking to the measuring cup.

Hazel Rumney's Mom's Yeast Rolls

MAKES ABOUT 1½ TO 2 DOZEN ROLLS

For all the years that I was growing up, my mother made yeast rolls. They were awesome and usually would not last a day. She didn't use a recipe and rarely measured anything. Of course, I tried to calculate her recipe by measuring out the ingredients and then re-measuring what was left after she finished. Mine don't seem to taste as good as the ones Mom used to make.

1 package yeast
½ cup lukewarm water
1 cup milk
¼ cup shortening
¼ cup sugar
2 teaspoons salt
1½ cups cold water
6 cups bread flour

Place the yeast in a small bowl and add the water to dissolve. Set aside.

Place the milk in a large saucepan and heat over medium heat until bubbles form around the edges—do not boil. Remove from the heat.

Add the shortening to the milk and stir to blend. Add the sugar and salt, and mix well. Add the water, then stir in the yeast mixture.

Place the flour in a large mixing bowl and add the other ingredients to it. Mix until completely blended. Cover and let rise 2 to 3 hours in a warm room.

Punch the dough down. Shape into rolls or larger size for buns. I remember Mom dipping her fingers in vegetable oil, pulling off a piece of dough, shaping it into a bun, and placing it in the bread pan.

Loosely cover the rolls and allow to rise for about 30 minutes.

Bake the rolls at 350°F for about 30 minutes, until golden brown.

Lucia Robson's Jalapeño Buttermilk Corn Muffins

MAKES 22 MUFFINS

My dad was from Georgia, so we had cornbread a lot in our house. The only seasoning we ever used, however, was salt. So the jalapeño corn muffin recipe is a salute to my dad, with an added kick for my jaded taste buds.

Preheat the oven to 400°F. Butter 22 medium-size muffin cups.

Combine the cornmeal, flour, baking soda, and salt. Stir in the corn, jalapeños, and cheese.

In another bowl, combine the oil, eggs, and buttermilk. Add this to the corn mixture, stirring only until the mixture is moistened. Do not overmix.

Fill the prepared muffin cups with the batter. Bake for 20 minutes, or until the muffins are golden brown.

3 tablespoons butter, for greasing the muffin tins
2 cups cornmeal
1 cup all-purpose flour
1 teaspoon baking soda
1 teaspoon salt
2 cups cream-style corn
4 fresh jalapeño peppers, seeded and chopped (more or fewer, to taste)
½ pound sharp white cheddar cheese, grated
½ cup olive oil (I actually use canola oil . . . don't much like olive.)
4 eggs, lightly beaten
2 cups buttermilk

Rocky Gibbons's Arizona Cornbread

SERVES 9

The basis for this recipe comes from a 1970 Albers Corn Meal contest I found while in high school in Arizona. I modified it to include one of my favorite taste sensations, cayenne pepper! It's a moist, comforting cornbread that's almost a casserole. Great with chili!

1 cup yellow cornmeal
½ teaspoon baking soda
1 teaspoon salt
¼ teaspoon ground red
    pepper (cayenne)
⅓ cup shortening
2 eggs
¾ cup milk
2 cups (1 15-ounce can)
    cream-style corn
1 cup (4 ounces) cheddar
    cheese, grated
1 (4-ounce) can diced
    green chiles, drained

Preheat the oven to 400°F.

Sift the dry ingredients into a bowl. Cut in the shortening until it is well blended.

Beat the eggs and milk together, then mix them with the dry ingredients. Add the cream-style corn to the mixture and blend it in.

Pour half of the mixture into a well-greased 8-inch square pan or a 9-inch cast iron skillet or baking dish. Top this with the grated cheese and green chiles, and pour the remainder of the cornmeal mixture over the cheese and chiles.

Bake the cornbread for about 30 minutes.

Susan Cummins Miller's Mesquite Cornbread

SERVES 6–9, DEPENDING ON THE SIZE OF THE SLICE

I love to use local and regional dishes as sensory elements in my Frankie MacFarlane mysteries. In *Detachment Fault*, I introduce Elena Navarro who, in addition to her day job at Dain Investigations, publishes cookbooks with native Sonoran recipes (which I create). When we meet her, she's fine-tuning a mesquite cornbread recipe by testing several variations on Frankie and her love interest, Philo Dain. This version was their favorite.

Preheat the oven to 350°F. Grease an 8 x 8-inch baking pan (or use cooking spray).

Combine the flour, cornmeal, mesquite flour, baking powder, baking soda, and salt in a medium-size bowl.

Combine the milk, eggs, oil, and nectar, honey, or sugar in a small bowl.

Add the wet ingredients to the dry ingredients, stirring with a spatula or wooden spoon until just combined. Spread the batter in the pan and let stand for 10 minutes.

Bake the cornbread for 20 to 25 minutes, until golden brown.

1 cup all-purpose flour
¾ cup cornmeal (yellow or blue)
¼ cup mesquite flour★
1 tablespoon baking powder
½ teaspoon baking soda
½ teaspoon salt
1 cup milk or buttermilk
2 large eggs
¼ cup vegetable oil
2 tablespoons agave nectar, honey, or sugar

★ I make my own mesquite flour by grinding dried pods from my honey mesquite trees, but it can be found online or at stores selling ingredients for Mexican food.

Sandy Whiting's Four-Alarm Batter Bread (aka Crazy Dog's Bread)

MAKES 1 LOAF

I gave this bread the above names for a reason. First off, every time I turn my oven up to 450°F and don't have an outside door open and at least one fan blowing, the oven heat sets off all four fire alarms in my house. The fire alarms then set off my two dogs into a barking, howling frenzy! It's total chaos for several minutes.

1½ cups milk, warmed
3 tablespoons extra-virgin olive oil
1 large egg, beaten
½ teaspoon salt
2¾ cups all-purpose flour
1 cup bread flour
¼ cup whole-wheat flour
3 tablespoons plus 1 teaspoon granulated sugar
1 tablespoon powdered milk
½ teaspoon cream of tartar
1 package yeast
½ teaspoon olive oil, for brushing on loaves

Mix the milk, olive oil, and egg until just blended.

In a separate bowl, combine all the dry ingredients and stir until blended. Add the mixed dry ingredients to the liquids and stir until well blended.

Let the dough rise about 30 minutes. Divide the dough in half. Spray two 9-inch round cake pans with nonstick cooking spray. Place each of the dough halves into a pan, pushing the dough out to the pans' edges. Brush ¼ teaspoon olive oil onto each loaf.

Bake the loaves at 450°F for exactly 12 minutes. Turn the bread onto a cutting board to cool.

Bread flour is best for baking bread because of its higher gluten content.

Sandy Whiting's Overnight Dutch Oven Bread

MAKES 1 LOAF

Just don't have time to bake? This recipe is for the lazy and/or harried baker. Literally throw together the ingredients in a large, warmed bowl at night (or before heading off to work), stir to combine, then bake either the next day or when just home from work. This is an excellent addition to any soup!

In a bowl, combine the flours, salt, and yeast. Stir in the water until it is just mixed. Be careful not to overwork the dough. Tightly cover the bowl and let it sit overnight at room temperature (between 70 and 85°F). In the morning, the dough will resemble a big bowl of foam. Not to worry!

Place a Dutch oven in the oven at 450°F and heat it.

With floured hands, form the dough into a ball and let it rest while the oven continues to heat. Gently place the dough into the Dutch oven (parchment paper can be placed in the bottom of the pot to prevent sticking). Bake the dough covered for 30 minutes. Uncover it and bake an additional 15 minutes. The top of the bread should be crusty and brown.

2¼ cups all-purpose flour
¾ cup whole-wheat flour
1½ teaspoons kosher salt
¾ teaspoon dry yeast
1½ cups warm water

Sandy Whiting's Pear and Cheese Salad

SERVES 4

Yummy from the get-go! This is a very light salad that presents well on individual salad plates. It also won a Blue Ribbon at the Kansas State Fair!

For the salad:
Large lettuce leaves
3 pears, preferable the red
ones, thinly sliced
Salt, to taste
6 ounces Brie (or other
mild cheese), chopped
½ cup pumpkin seeds,
shelled
Red onion rings, for
garnish

For the dressing:
3 tablespoons canola oil
1 tablespoon tarragon
vinegar
Dash of hot pepper sauce

Wash and dry the lettuce leaves and arrange them on individual salad plates. Place the pears on the lettuce. Lightly salt the Brie and sprinkle it over the pears. Sprinkle the pumpkin seeds over the Brie.

Whisk together the dressing ingredients and pour the dressing over the salad. Garnish the salad with red onion rings.

Susan D. Matley's "Hands On" Spinach Salad

SERVES QUITE A FEW

Years ago, I was faced with attending a Christmas pig roast. Call me a wimp, but I've never been thrilled about carving my dinner right off the carcass. Aside from the pig (roasted on a spit in cold, rainy Seattle by six stout fellows with a jug of whiskey), the event was potluck. This recipe is how I joined in on the primitive festivities.

First and foremost, thoroughly WASH YOUR HANDS.

In a large salad bowl, WITH YOUR BARE HANDS, toss the spinach, onions, and oranges. Drain the artichoke hearts, reserving the liquid. Chop the artichoke hearts, and WITH YOUR BARE HANDS, sprinkle them on top of the salad mixture.

WITH YOUR BARE HANDS, crumble the blue cheese on top of the artichoke hearts. Pour the reserved artichoke heart marinade over all, and toss WITH YOUR BARE HANDS until well mixed.

Note: After the tough guys who had roasted the pig finished shrieking, "Eeeewww! You tossed that WITH YOUR BARE HANDS!" we all settled down to a fine Christmas feast.

2 bunches spinach, washed and stems removed

1 bunch green onions, thinly sliced

4 fresh mandarin or other small oranges, peeled, seeded, and chopped

2 jars marinated artichoke hearts (the short, square type of jars)

1 healthy wedge blue cheese

Get in the chair and write on a regular schedule.

Stay open to new ideas.

Mindfully consider constructive criticism and act on advice that you determine to be good!

Always, always thank your readers.

Sharon Magee's Tortellini Broccoli Salad

SERVES 10–15

Years ago the cafeteria in the company where I was employed served a pasta salad that I loved. I decided to try to replicate it. It's gone through many iterations over the years, and here is the result—very different from the original. This has become one of my most requested dishes. When family visits and I ask what they'd like to eat, invariably this salad is in the mix.

3 large broccoli crowns
2 (1-pound, 4-ounce) packages refrigerated tortellini, any flavor
2 large tomatoes
1 large sweet onion
1 (6.5-ounce) pepperoni stick
1 (3.8-ounce) can sliced black olives, drained
Creamy Italian dressing

Blanch the broccoli crowns in boiling salted water. Drain them, crown-side down, on paper towels.

Cook the tortellini in salted water, following package instructions. Drain.

Cut the broccoli, tomatoes, and onion into bite-size pieces. Cut the pepperoni stick into ¼- to ½-inch slices, then cut those in half.

Combine the olives and all the other ingredients with the creamy Italian dressing.

For the best flavor, refrigerate the salad for several hours, or overnight. It can be served as a side or main dish.

Audrey Smith's Hot Day Melon Salad, contributed by Brad Smith

SERVES 12

This recipe has its roots in traditional Mexican fruit salad. It is prepared fresh and served on Field Day for our small local school (under a hundred students for grades kindergarten through eighth). On Field Day, students, parents, and locals gather for a fun end-of-school activity. The weather is usually very warm and windy. After competitive events, the participants are ready for an all-you-can-eat buffet that includes many homemade dishes. This fresh recipe is a favorite.

Combine the dressing ingredients until the sugar dissolves.

Clean the melons and cut them into bite-size pieces, removing the rinds. Peel the cucumbers and cut them into similar sizes. Add the onion and cilantro. Add the dressing and toss the salad.

Marinate the salad overnight in the refrigerator. Serve chilled.

For the salad:
1 honeydew melon
1 cantaloupe melon
2 cucumbers
½ cup diced red onion
¼ cup chopped cilantro

For the dressing:
1 cup unseasoned rice
   vinegar
½ cup water
¼ cup sugar
1 jalapeño pepper, minced

As for writing, my wife insists she is going to get me a cap that says: Sit down, shut up, and write! I also write the books that are missing from my shelf.

Nancy Plain's Sweet and Tangy Cranberry Relish

SERVES A LOT OF PEOPLE (A LITTLE BIT GOES A LONG WAY)

I serve this easy-to-make cranberry relish to my large family group every Thanksgiving. Over the years, I've fiddled with the recipe and finally found just the right balance of flavors, a little bit tart, a little bit sweet. I always cook up a batch a couple of weeks before the holiday and freeze it in two or three containers. Any relish left over is great with roast chicken and many other chicken or turkey dishes. Full disclosure: A couple of family members still prefer the canned kind (it comes out of the can in that perfect cylinder and slices so neatly!), so I always stock up on that, too.

3 Granny Smith apples,
   peeled, cored, and diced
2–3 ripe pears, peeled,
   cored, and diced
2 pounds fresh cranberries
   (or an approximate
   amount in bags)
1 cup raisins (optional)
2 cups sugar
1 cup orange juice
2 teaspoons cinnamon
¼ teaspoon nutmeg
2 tablespoons grated
   orange rind

Mix all the ingredients together in a large pot and bring to a boil. Simmer uncovered for about 45 minutes. Let the relish cool before freezing, or serve it fresh.

If you are lucky enough to have a beloved dog, sit that dog right by your side while you write. If you don't have one, think about rescuing your new best friend from your local shelter. You'll never get lonely while you work.

Vicky Rose's Cornbread Salad

SERVES 10

While driving through East Texas, a friend and I stopped at a little diner in a small town. On their buffet, they had an unusual salad I'd never seen before. I learned that it was created by a chef somewhere in the South to use up old cornbread. It tasted so good that I searched until I found the right combination of recipes for it. I've taken it to potlucks and have found it is something people are a little afraid to try. Most people who try it like it just fine, but there are always one or two who love it and gorge on it.

Crumble the cornbread into a large bowl and add the other ingredients, stirring well. You can add a little salt and pepper, but be careful because the bacon will be salty, too. Refrigerate until the cornbread salad is served. It tastes better the next day.

An 8 x 8-inch pan of your favorite cooked cornbread, or leftover cornbread to approximate that amount

12 slices bacon, fried and crumbled (For more bacon flavor, fry the whole package.)

1 medium onion, finely chopped

1 green bell pepper, finely chopped (optional)

2 large tomatoes or 4 small ones, chopped

1 (15-ounce) can whole kernel corn, drained (optional)

1½ cups mayonnaise, or more to suit your taste and according to the amount of cornbread you have (In the South, Duke's is preferred.)

Salt and pepper, to taste

Some of the best advice I have comes from other writers, and I'm paraphrasing them here. From Michael Blake, author, actor, and special effects makeup artist: Don't try to write to fit a trend or what you think is popular at the time. It won't ring true. Write from the heart. From Spur winners John Nesbitt and Michael Blakely: Make your manuscript as clean and as grammatically correct as you can. Don't expect an editor to clean it up for you. Even if it's a masterpiece, they will never know it because they won't read past the first paragraph. And don't expect another author to use his influence with his publisher to help you get published. That kind of influence doesn't exist. From movie director Courtney Joyner on screenplays: Don't have people just standing around talking. Have them doing something. Put them in action. Focus on the main character and have him or her in every scene. From two-time Spur finalist Carol Crigger: Just write.

Vicky Rose's Cucumber Salad

SERVES 4–5

This recipe was passed down to me by my aunt Ludwena Hilscher. There is no telling how old this simple recipe is, and unfortunately, I neglected to ask my aunt where she obtained it. Aunt Ludwena was an old maid who lived in Austin and worked at one time for the University of Texas cafeteria. The recipe probably came from one of her coworkers. When UT closed its cafeteria, the workers were allowed to split up the restaurant-ware, which had an unusual pattern of chuck-wagons and cattle brands on it. Eating off those dishes at my aunt's house helped foster my love for all things Western.

Peel and slice the cucumbers. Bring to a boil the sugar, vegetable oil, vinegar, and salt. Pour the boiling mixture over the cucumbers and refrigerate.

Note: I've tried using wine vinegar in this recipe, but white vinegar tastes better. And I never get fancy with the oil either.

3 large salad cucumbers or
  6 smaller pickling ones
¾ cup sugar
⅓ cup vegetable oil
⅓ cup plain white vinegar
Dash of salt

JoJo Thoreau's Olive Wrangler's Salad

SERVES 2–4

My mom will not be surprised to hear me say this is one of my favorite recipes because she already calls me an olive wrangler. Olives have always been a favorite snack of mine, so this side dish has become a family favorite (or at least a JoJo favorite). My favorite time of year to enjoy this chilled side dish is in the summer while we are camping. However, if you notice that your bowl of salad begins to lose many of its chopped olives, then I would dare say that you have an olive wrangler in your midst as well.

Note: JoJo is our youngest WWA member at age ten and has already written two books, including *Buckaroo Bobbie Sue,* that won a 2016 Spur Award.

1 (5-7 ounce) jar Manzanilla pimento stuffed olives, drained and chopped

1 (6.5-ounce) can black olives, drained and chopped

2 celery stalks, chopped

1 pound cherry tomatoes, cut in half, or 2–3 large tomatoes, diced

½ teaspoon minced garlic

2 tablespoons flaxseed oil or olive oil

In a medium to large bowl, combine the olives, celery, tomatoes, and garlic. Drizzle with oil; toss to coat.

Cover and refrigerate for 4 hours or overnight.

Note: You can use any type of olive in this salad, and if you have an abundance of cucumbers in your garden as well as tomatoes, you can add 1 pound of diced cucumbers.

JoJo Thoreau's Delightful Carrot Sticks

SERVES 2–4

This recipe is especially fun to make in the summertime when you have a plentiful carrot crop in your garden. I have always enjoyed orange juice as well as carrots, but before trying this recipe, I would have never believed having them at the same time would be so delicious! And, if you're looking for a fun and simple side dish that your little buckaroos can help prepare, I highly recommend this one. Spoiler alert, sometimes when us young buckaroos have a hand in preparing the grub, we're more likely to enjoy eating it (even when it contains vegetables)!

Cook the carrots in a small amount of water in a saucepan, covered, until they are tender.

While the carrots are cooking, use another saucepan to combine the brown sugar and cornstarch. Stir in the orange juice until the mixture is smooth, and bring it to a soft boil. Cook and stir for about 2 minutes, until it's thickened and bubbly, then stir in the butter.

Drain your carrots and top with the orange juice mixture to enjoy as a side dish.

1 pound carrots, julienned
1 tablespoon brown sugar
1 teaspoon cornstarch
¼ cup orange juice
2 tablespoons butter

Sandra McGee's Southwest Slaw

SERVES 8–10

The long list of ingredients may suggest a lot of prep work. However, after a frustrating day at my laptop, unable to cross one thing off that day's writing projects, it feels good to put on an apron and accomplish something in the kitchen. I line up all the ingredients on the counter in the order the recipe calls for, and barrel through. In no time, I have a delicious slaw. Goes well with Bill McGee's Award-Winning Chili.

For the sauce:
½ cup mayonnaise
½ cup plain yogurt
⅛ cup chile sauce
2 tablespoons horseradish
2 tablespoons Dijon mustard
1 tablespoon Worcestershire sauce
¼ cup apple cider vinegar
2 tablespoons lemon juice
Salt and pepper, to taste

1 pound Savoy cabbage, core removed and thinly sliced
¼ pound regular green cabbage, core removed and thinly sliced
¼ pound red cabbage, core removed and thinly sliced
½ cup celery, thinly sliced on the bias
½ bunch green onions, thinly sliced on the bias
¼ cup walnut pieces, roughly chopped
½ cup blue cheese, crumbled

Combine all the ingredients for the sauce. Allow it to stand for 30 minutes.

Combine the vegetables with the right amount of sauce and toss the slaw.

"The strongest drive is neither love nor hate; it is the urge to change another's copy." (From a sign posted on the bulletin board in the Department of Journalism, Ball State University.)

Natalie Bright's Maw's Cherry Salad

SERVES 10

My grandmother, Iylene Shuffield Williams, made this sweet cherry salad as a side for the turkey at every family gathering. A unique lead-crystal bowl held the fluffy creation. One taste and I'm transported back to my grandparents' cotton farm. I can hear the buzz of cicadas as we shelled black-eyed peas under the giant elms. When I set the same bowl on my table, my grandmother's smile and the smells of her kitchen flitter through my memory. Sometimes the taste of food passes over your tongue and drifts into your heart, where it remains forever. This cherry fluff recipe has been around forever. Instead of using Eagle Brand Sweetened Condensed Milk, I created a much lower calorie version. I included both recipes.

Mix all the ingredients together, cover, and chill 2 hours before serving.

Natalie's lower-calorie version:
2 (6-ounce) cartons Greek yogurt vanilla
1 (20-ounce) can lite cherry pie filling, no sugar added
1 (15-ounce) can pineapple tidbits (in their own juice), drained
1 (8-ounce) container sugar-free Cool Whip

Optional additions:
1 cup nuts, chopped
1 cup miniature marshmallows
¼ cup coconut, shredded

Original recipe:
1 can sweetened condensed milk
1 can cherry pie filling
1 large can pineapple tidbits, drained
1 large container whipped topping

Write the story that keeps waking you up at night. Don't be afraid of the ideas that pop into your head.

Place a coconut in the oven until it is warm, then crack it open with only a slight blow. The milk will be delicious, and the coconut meat will separate easily from the shell.

Gloria Markley's Deviled Eggs, contributed by Bill Markley

MAKES 48

Deviled eggs! I love deviled eggs. If you set out deviled eggs, I'll eat them all! When I was in my teens, making hay was a family event, when we traveled to all the relatives' farms. The men and boys would be out slinging bales onto the wagons, stacking them, then unloading and stacking them in the barns while my mom and aunts would bring us ice-cold sweet tea. At lunch, we'd sit on a cool porch and feast on a variety of foods, including—deviled eggs. Here's Mom's own deviled egg concoction. Bet you can't eat just one!

2 dozen hard-boiled eggs
1 teaspoon dried mustard
2 tablespoons vinegar
1 teaspoon salt
¼ cup sugar
¼ cup mayonnaise

Slice the eggs and remove the yolks, mashing the yolks while they are still warm.

Add all the other ingredients to the mashed yolks and mix well.

Fill the egg whites with the mixture.

Eat.

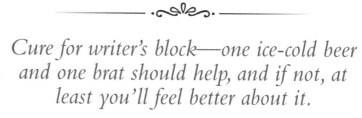

Cure for writer's block—one ice-cold beer and one brat should help, and if not, at least you'll feel better about it.

Jennifer Smith-Mayo and Matthew Mayo's Team Gritty Lip-Smackin' Applesauce

SERVES 4–6 HUNGRY CRITTERS!

This Team Gritty recipe is simple, wholesome, and tasty. It's also ideal to make just about any-where—with apples freshly harvested from the orchard on our Maine farmstead, or with apples bought at a farmers' market in Livingston, Montana! As Team Gritty (aka award-winning photographer and videographer Jennifer Smith-Mayo and Spur Award–winning author Matthew P. Mayo), we run Gritty Press (www.GrittyPress.com) and travel all over the US map in search of hot coffee, tasty whiskey, and high adventure. We spend most of our time roving the West, writing and researching books, hiking, photographing, and, yes, eating good local food—such as applesauce!

Place the apple pieces in a sturdy pot (a Dutch oven works great). Sprinkle the grated lemon rind and lemon juice over the apples. Stir to mix. Drizzle with the water.

Cook for about 1 hour on medium-low heat and stir occasionally, until the apples become soft (cooking time varies and depends on the firmness and type of apple). If the apple pieces get too dry, add a few more tablespoons of water to prevent them from sticking to the bottom of the pot.

At the end, when the apples are soft and tender, stir in the cinnamon. Add more cinnamon if desired.

For smooth applesauce, puree the apples in the pot with a stick blender, or use a blender to process the applesauce in small batches. (Careful, they're hot!) For a chunky sauce, mash the apples with a fork, potato masher, or handheld mixer.

Serve the applesauce hot or cold. And most of all . . . enjoy!

2–3 pounds apples, cored, peeled (if desired), and cut into chunks or slices

1–2 tablespoons fresh grated lemon rind (if desired)

2–3 tablespoons fresh-squeezed lemon juice

½ cup water

½–1 teaspoon cinnamon

Anne Hillerman's Crispy Avocado Moons

SERVES 6–8

This is a nice side dish with a steak and a salad or a great starter for company. You can serve it as an appetizer with salsa, pico de gallo, or a touch of sour cream. In a pinch, you can keep them hot in the oven until your overdue company arrives. Or start without the latecomers and let them finish off the salsa with those tortilla chips you've been saving for emergencies.

2 quarts vegetable oil for deep frying
4 small ripe avocados
¾ cup panko (Japanese bread crumbs)
Salt and pepper
1 cup flour
4 eggs, beaten

Heat the cooking oil in a deep pan to about 350°F.

Cut the avocados in half and remove the pits. Cut them again into quarters or eighths, depending on your own preference. Peel the avocado slices.

Mix the panko, salt, and pepper in a bowl.

Dredge the peeled avocado slices in the flour, then in the eggs, and then in the panko mixture. Fry them until crispy and golden brown, about 1 minute. Serve them at once.

Writing, at least for me, goes better when I can keep to a regular schedule. Just like setting time aside for exercise or meditation, a daily plan for writing keeps the writing muscles toned and flexible.

Details are important, but use them judiciously. Don't let setting the scene, costumes, or backstory get in the way of the central plot. (Yes, I have trouble with this one!) In fiction, details add the juice, but they aren't the whole watermelon. Readers have imaginations and like to use them. Challenge them to fill in a few blanks. Nonfiction authors have more leeway in terms of inserting more of those juicy details, but even then you need to remember the big picture.

Creating stories, or taking facts and arranging them as nonfiction narrative, is supposed to be enjoyable as well as challenging. Every non-writing job I've had came with good days and bad, and the same is true of the writing life. Sometimes, the words flow and characters practically dictate the story. Sometimes, writing is hard work. Remember those good days when you're struggling with the difficult ones.

Glenna's Banana-Pecan Salad, contributed by Robert Yoho

SERVES 4–6

This salad recipe was originally used by my mother, who often made it for our family during the holidays. After she passed away in 2003, I figured it was something else lost to me, especially since Mom never wrote anything down and cooked without measuring. In order to surprise me, my wife played around with the dish until she closely duplicated the taste. Like another one of my late mother's dishes I reproduced, whenever I eat it, it reminds me of her. It also reminds me how blessed I am to have had these two wonderful women in my life.

1 head lettuce
2 bananas, sliced
1 cup (or so) pecans
½ cup Miracle Whip
3 tablespoons milk
3 tablespoons sugar

After chopping the lettuce, add the bananas and pecans. (I prefer a few more pecans, but add as few or as many as you like.) To make the salad dressing, combine the Miracle Whip, milk, and sugar in a pint jar. Cover the jar with a lid, shake it to blend the ingredients, and then pour the dressing over your salad. Mix and enjoy!

*As for writing . . . Books are like children.
They are often conceived by inspiration,
but they are born only by labor.*

Neil (aka Montana Kid Hammer) Wetherington's Texian Chuckwagon-Style Greens

SERVES 6–8

The Golden Heart Shootist Society, a chapter of the Single Action Shootist Society, meets in Fairbanks, Alaska. As a member, I attend the club's annual Memorial Day weekend shooting event, called "Cow-boy Camp." There a gathering of cowboys and cowgirls meet to shoot and to "vittles up" around the chuckwagon campfire. This is my very favorite recipe to prepare at camp as my contribution to my Cowboy Action Shooting family. Ever since I was a youngster, greens of this kind have always been one of my preferred side dishes.

Boil the water in a pot or kettle, then add the salt and cut greens. Bring the contents to a medium simmer. If cooking with meat, add it now, along with the black pepper and onions. Stir this gently from time to time.

Next add the crushed red peppers and garlic, and either the chili pepper, red cayenne, or paprika, to taste. Stir again gently, so as not to damage the greens as they soften. Cook until the greens are tender to your liking.

Remove the pot or kettle from the heat and add the chopped chives. Let the chives steep for 5 minutes, and then serve. The vinegar may be added during this 5-minute resting time or after the dish is served, according to cookie's preference. Sesame or poppy seeds may also be added when served.

1 gallon water

2–3 pinches sea salt

8 bundles kale, mustard, or collard greens, washed well and cut into strips

½–1 pound cooked chicken bits or bacon strips (optional)

1 big pinch black pepper, freshly ground

1 handful dehydrated onions

1 big pinch dehydrated crushed red peppers

1–2 medium pinches garlic powder or crushed garlic extract

1 big pinch ground chili pepper, ground red cayenne pepper, or paprika

1–2 handfuls fresh chives, chopped

1–2 tablespoons apple cider vinegar (optional)

Sesame or poppy seeds, to taste (optional)

Cheewa James's Broccoli and Cheese Casserole

SERVES 4–6

When my sons Todd and Dave were boys, there were certain things they did not like: broccoli, spinach—well, the usual list of foods kids tend to dislike. So I came up with a casserole that had broccoli in it. Those boys loved that casserole, and I managed to smuggle some broccoli into their diets. We just didn't mention the word broccoli when we talked about it. It was called "Mama's Green and Yellow Yummy." It is now "Cheewa's Broccoli and Cheese Casserole." Funny thing is, it tastes exactly the same.

1 cup mayonnaise
1 cup grated cheese, your
  choice
2 eggs
1 (22–23-ounce) can cream
  of mushroom soup
2–3 cups fresh broccoli, or
  1 (16-ounce) package
  frozen broccoli

Preheat the oven to 350°F.

Mix together the mayonnaise, cheese, eggs, and soup.

If you are using fresh broccoli, microwave it 1½ minutes. If you are using frozen broccoli, cook 5 minutes on the stove. Fold the broccoli into the other mixed ingredients.

Bake the casserole for 45 minutes.

Don't tell me there is a storm; let me hear the branch smashing the window and the dog howling in alarm.

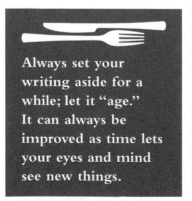

Always set your writing aside for a while; let it "age." It can always be improved as time lets your eyes and mind see new things.

Carol Crigger's Triple Corn Casserole

SERVES 6–8

Corn is not my favorite veggie, although this could make me change my mind. I've finally found and amended a recipe that satisfies everyone in my family, including me, who just so happens to be the cook. Is this casserole good for you? I'm pretty sure the calories add up, but the main criteria are met. It tastes good and is filling. If you're a real stickler for freshness, it is possible to cream your own corn and to sift together dry ingredients for a half-recipe of cornbread. Be sure to use the smoked variety of paprika, otherwise you might as well leave it out.

Preheat the oven to 350°F.

Mix all the ingredients together except the cheese, and pour the mixture into a greased baking dish.

After the casserole has baked for 45 minutes, or is set in the middle and golden brown, sprinkle it with the cheese and put it back in the oven. Let the cheese melt, take the casserole out, and enjoy this ridiculously buttery dish.

1 cup whole-kernel sweet corn, fresh off the cob or frozen and thawed
1 (15-ounce) can cream-style corn
1 (8-ounce) package corn muffin mix
1 cup sour cream
½ cup butter, melted
2 tablespoons fresh chives, snipped
1 teaspoon chili powder
1 teaspoon smoked paprika, or to taste
1 cup cheddar (or your favorite) cheese, shredded

David Morrell's Rambo's Daddy's Doctored Pinto Beans

SERVES 4–6

Because my novel, *First Blood*, is a Western in disguise, I can't resist naming this fast recipe after Rambo, the gunfighter who wants to retire but isn't allowed to. I live in Santa Fe, the elevation of which is around 7,000 feet. Boiling pinto beans until they're soft takes forever here, unless I use a pressure cooker, but Rambo seldom has a pressure cooker, so here's his rapid way of cooking pinto beans around a campfire. They're wonderful with burgers, ribs, and barbecued chicken or else on their own in a tortilla. Rambo, of course, prefers to eat these beans with wild boar. Although Rambo is strong, these beans are mild if smaller amounts of spice are used.

2 tablespoons olive oil
1 medium sweet onion, coarsely chopped
1 clove garlic, peeled and left whole (If the cloves are small, use two.)
1 (32-ounce) can, or 2 (15-ounce) cans, plain pinto beans, undrained (Rambo uses his knife as a can opener.)
½ (8-ounce) can tomato sauce (Freeze leftover sauce in a baggie for future use—Rambo is frugal, but alas, he's able to do this only in a snow cave during winter.)
2 slices bacon, snipped into small "bean-size" pieces (Precooked is quick, but if not precooked, fry gently and drain.)
½ teaspoon chipotle chile powder (Use ¼ teaspoon if children or those sensitive to spices are joining the meal—Rambo is always kind to children and the weak.)
½ teaspoon ground cumin (Again, use ¼ teaspoon if children or those sensitive to spices are joining the meal.)
½ bay leaf
½ cup water
Salt and pepper, to taste

In a medium saucepan, add the olive oil over low to medium heat. Add the chopped onion and whole garlic clove(s). Sauté and slowly "sweat" until softened. (As Rambo's muscles indicate, he believes in sweating.)

Add undrained pinto beans and all the other ingredients. Stir and bring to a medium boil and then cover the pot, but leave the lid slightly open. Stew 40 to 45 minutes, stirring occasionally. Remove garlic clove(s) and bay leaf, and serve.

Like the ingredients in this recipe, the more senses an author appeals to, the more a story will feel multidimensional.

Ann Noble's Baked Beans

SERVES ABOUT 18–20

Here at the Cora Valley Angus Ranch, in Cora, Wyoming, I usually serve fifty for lunch every branding. My meal has become standard over the years, and consists of barbecued beef ribs, baked beans, coleslaw, potato and onion casserole, cornbread and honey butter, and a table full of desserts. I always hope it doesn't rain, not only so the job of branding gets done, but because the workers can eat outside. I have enough to clean with all the dishes, and I'm always thankful when I don't have to clean all the chairs! Here is my baked beans recipe.

12 slices bacon
2 pounds ground beef
1 large onion, peeled and chopped
3 (16-ounce) cans baked beans
3 (16-ounce) cans butter beans
3 (16-ounce) cans kidney beans
1 cup ketchup
1½ cups packed brown sugar
¼ cup Worcestershire sauce

Preheat the oven to 350°F.

In a large skillet over medium heat, fry the bacon. Drain it on a paper towel, let it cool, and then crumble it and set it aside.

Add the ground beef and onion to the bacon fat in the pan, and cook until the meat is browned. Put the meat, onion, and bacon into a large roasting pan and add the remaining ingredients. Bake for a couple of hours, stirring occasionally.

Cotton Smith's Good Anytime Baked Beans

SERVES UP TO 18

This recipe was submitted by the Smith family in Cotton's honor. They wrote, "For Cotton, it wasn't so much about the food, it was where he was and the people he was with that delighted him. He had a passion for life that brought happiness to anyone blessed to be near him. This was a favorite dish of his, especially in summer, surrounded by family, laughter, good times, and a cigar. Oh, and don't forget the grilled brats."

Adjust the oven rack to lower-middle position and preheat the oven to 325°F.

Fry the bacon in large skillet on medium heat until it is partially cooked (half cooked) and has released about ¼ cup drippings.

Remove the bacon from the pan and drain on paper towels. Add the onion (and peppers if you wish) to the bacon grease in the pan and sauté until tender, about 5 minutes.

Add the beans, barbeque sauce, brown sugar, and mustard to the pan and bring to a simmer. (If the skillet is not large enough, add just the beans and heat to a simmer, then transfer to a large bowl and stir in remaining ingredients.)

Pour the flavored beans into an ovenproof pan or crock. Top with the bacon, then bake until the beans are bubbly, the bacon is brown, and the sauce is the consistency of pancake syrup, about 2 hours. Let stand to thicken slightly and serve.

8 slices bacon, cut into 2 pieces
1 medium onion, diced
½ medium green pepper, diced (optional)
1 small jalapeño pepper, diced (optional)
3 (28-ounce) cans pork and beans, drained
¾–1 cup barbecue sauce (You decide, to taste. The Smith family likes 1 cup of KC Masterpiece Original sauce.)
½ cup brown sugar
2 teaspoons Dijon or regular yellow mustard (You decide, to taste.)

Sherry Monahan's Sweet Potato Casserole

SERVES 6, UNLESS MY NIECE AND NEPHEW ARE JOINING YOU!

I've been making this recipe for over fifteen years for every holiday. My niece Tiffany and nephew Alex got really ticked when one Thanksgiving I didn't make it. So now I religiously make "SPC," as they call it, or fear their wrath! It's so dang good, I wonder why I don't make it year-round. It would make a nice dessert, too.

3 cups mashed sweet potatoes
½ stick butter, room temperature
1 egg, beaten
2 teaspoons vanilla extract
¼ cup white sugar
¼ cup brown sugar
¼ cup (4 tablespoons) butter, room temperature
½ cup pecan pieces

Grease a 9 x 11-inch pan or something similar. Preheat the oven to 375°F.

Combine the potatoes, butter, egg, vanilla, and white sugar in a bowl and mix well. Place in baking pan.

In a separate bowl, crumble the brown sugar, butter, and pecans for the topping. Sprinkle all over the sweet potato mixture and bake for about 20 to 30 minutes or until golden.

G. R. (Honest Doc) Williamson's Prescott's Potatoes

SERVES 4–6

We Texans owe a lot to ol' W. P. Webb. He was the reason most of us got interested in Texas history. Somehow this seems like a dish that would have been developed in the French Quarter to honor the refined history professor. Sort of like a "Potatoes Benedict," you might say. Yeah, he probably would've liked that, being as he was the scholarly type who liked everything prim and proper. You can just picture him sitting down to a finely set table, with a white napkin across his lap, pushing his fork down through this luscious potato dish.

Sauté the potatoes in a large skillet, using a small amount of canola oil and seasoning. When the potatoes are tender to the touch, add the diced ham. Cover with a lid and cook on low heat for 5 minutes.

Place the potatoes and ham in a baking dish. Spread the shredded cheese over the top and place the dish in a warm oven until the cheese is melted and ready for the hollandaise sauce.

To make the sauce, stir the melted butter into the hollandaise sauce mix until it is smooth. Warm the cup of milk and whisk it into the mix. Microwave the mix for 1 minute, then remove it and whisk. Repeat this until the sauce thickens.

Pour the hollandaise sauce over the potatoes and serve the dish on a warmer.

1 package country-style hash brown potatoes
2 tablespoons canola oil
Salt (or seasoned salt) and pepper, to taste
1 cup diced ham
2 cups shredded Colby Jack cheese
1 packet hollandaise sauce mix
¼ cup butter, melted
1 cup milk

Michael Zimmer's Funeral Potatoes

SERVES 6–8

This is an old Utah standby, quick and easy to make, and a comforting staple during tragedies or celebrations. Or maybe both, depending on the deceased.

1 (10.75-ounce) can cream of chicken soup

¼ cup milk

1 cup sour cream

1 cup shredded cheese (Colby Jack tickles my fancy best, but any kind will do.)

1 teaspoon salt

¼ teaspoon pepper

4 cups frozen, shredded potatoes

Preheat the oven to 350°F.

Combine the ingredients and bake for 40 to 45 minutes, uncovered the last 15 minutes.

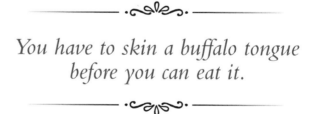

You have to skin a buffalo tongue before you can eat it.

Quackgrass Sally's Myrna's Marvelous Mashed Ranch Taters

SERVES 6–8 (OR 4 RANCH COWBOYS AND KITCHEN PORCH DOG)

My mom made this every Christmas Eve for my cowboys, and there were never any leftovers . . . the dog was lucky to lick the bowl afterwards! You can refrigerate or freeze this, too, for cooking later. I often put these potatoes into smaller loaf pans and freeze them. Then later on, I have yummy smaller portions for my cowboy, the dog, and me for supper. This reheats well in the microwave.

Preheat the oven to 350°F.

Combine all the ingredients in a large, deep oven-casserole bowl.

Bake for 30 to 40 minutes, until the middle is HOT. (Stir once in a while, if needed, during the heating.)

Remove the casserole from the oven, and serve up the potatoes by the ladleful!

5 pounds potatoes, cooked and mashed

8 ounces cream cheese, softened

1 cup half-and-half

1 stick margarine or butter, melted

1 tablespoon seasoned salt

1 teaspoon onion powder

1 teaspoon pepper

1 pinch garlic powder, if you like

Chapter Four

Come an' Get It! (Main Dishes)

If you're working on a book, you've probably been taxing your brain to the utmost, from morning until dusk. You've been staring into space, searching for the perfect word, the perfect organization, the perfect insight.

Nothing says "Stop working for the day!" when the cook in your house yells, "Come an' get it!" Well, OK, they're probably saying something like "Your dinner is getting cold" or "Are you ever coming out to eat?" If you're alone, then it's your stomach yelling the same thing at you.

We writers tend to hunker down and work for hours without a break or a meal. Why? It's because we usually wait until the last minute to finish our project. We believe that deadlines were made for writers because without them, we'd never be published!

Pour yourself a glass of wine and treat yourself to one of these hearty dinners. This is your reward.

Terry Del Bene's Holiday Oxtail Stew

SERVES 4–6

One of the dishes consumed by the Donner Party on Christmas was oxtail stew. Oxtail is a very tough cut of meat, and it says something about the scarcity of food that oxtail stew was celebratory fare. The version presented here likely is the oxtail stew they wished they were able to make.

I once was an instructor at a living history training session. The participants were divided into teams, and we encouraged competition between these divisions. All weekend long we dangled a rare prize, a delicacy meal prepared for the winning team. As the competition came to an end, the winners lorded their victory over the losers. I prepared buffalo tongue, a nineteenth-century delicacy appropriate to the study focus of the training. When a beautiful, tender, steaming-hot buffalo tongue was presented to the winners at their exclusive victory dinner, they looked at it with shocked expressions and said, "Can we share it with the others?"

1 onion, diced

4 tablespoons olive oil

2½ pounds oxtail, chopped into stew-size pieces

½ cup apple cider vinegar

Salt, to taste

Black pepper, to taste

Worcestershire sauce, to taste

Water (sufficient to completely cover the other ingredients)

2 cups diced celery

1 pound carrots, diced

3 pounds potatoes, cut into pieces double the size of the oxtail pieces

2 cups whole kernel corn

½ cup green peas

½ cup green beans

1 pint tomato puree

1 clove garlic, diced very fine

Rosemary spears, to taste

2 bay leaves

Chili powder (optional)

Cilantro (optional)

Hot sauce (optional)

Sauté the onion in the olive oil until it is caramelized.

Dip the oxtail meat in the apple cider vinegar, and sprinkle the salt, pepper, and Worcestershire sauce over the stew meat. Immediately sear the oxtail meat over a high-temperature fire until the exterior is lightly browned (this usually takes about 4 minutes).

Over moderate heat, place the water, browned oxtail meat, caramelized onion, celery, carrots, potatoes, corn, peas, green beans, tomato puree, garlic, and spices into a large covered pot. Bring the mixture to a rapid boil and allow it to boil for 30 minutes. Reduce the heat to a temperature sufficient to simmer the mixture. Simmer it overnight (a minimum of 6 hours, but no more than 10 hours). Be sure to stir the pot and sample the stew as you go so you can adjust the spices. You can make this recipe bolder by adding chili powder, cilantro, and/or hot sauce to taste.

Serve piping hot, and have a wonderful holiday.

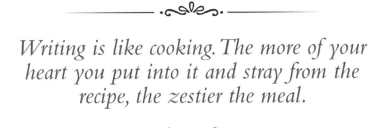

Writing is like cooking. The more of your heart you put into it and stray from the recipe, the zestier the meal.

Jim Jones's Texas Chili

SERVES 4–6

As a Texan living in New Mexico, it was hard to find anyone who could even spell chili correctly (they spell it with an e . . . chile), much less someone who could make honest-to-goodness Texas chili. I finally decided to just make my own. Since beer is involved in the recipe, I've been asked how I could eat after "all those beers." There's a very specific scientific formula about the ratio of portions of chili to Shiner Bock that allow you to keep functioning. Unfortunately, I can't remember the formula. Most importantly, there are no beans in Texas chili!

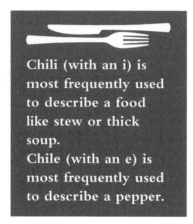

Chili (with an i) is most frequently used to describe a food like stew or thick soup.
Chile (with an e) is most frequently used to describe a pepper.

2 tablespoons olive oil
Garlic paste, to taste
1 onion, diced
2 pounds ground beef
1 pound hot sausage
½ teaspoon salt
½ teaspoon seasoned salt
1 teaspoon ground pepper
2 tablespoons red chili powder
1 tablespoon cayenne pepper
1 (28-ounce) can whole tomatoes
1 (10-ounce) can Ro-Tel tomatoes
1 (6-ounce) can tomato paste
¾ teaspoon cumin
2 teaspoons oregano
2 teaspoons paprika
¼ cup parsley, chopped
½ cup dark beer (Pour in ⅓ of a Shiner Bock, drink the rest.)
Hot sauce, to taste
Cheddar cheese, grated (optional)
Jalapeños (optional)
Green chiles (optional)
Pinto beans (optional)

In a large pot, heat the olive oil. Add the garlic paste and diced onion and sauté over medium heat for 5 minutes. Add the ground beef and sausage, brown until all redness is gone, and drain.

Season with the salt, seasoned salt, and ground pepper. Add the chili powder and cayenne pepper and cook for 2 more minutes.

Stir in the tomatoes, Ro-Tel tomatoes, tomato paste, cumin, oregano, paprika, parsley, and beer. Sprinkle liberally with hot sauce and stir.

Let the chili simmer for 2 to 3 hours. Taste it frequently. Stir it frequently. Drink another Shiner Bock.

Serve the chili in bowls. You may add the grated cheddar cheese, if desired. You may also add the jalapeños. You may even add the green chiles to assuage the guilt of New Mexicans who must come to terms with the fact they're enjoying something from Texas. You can even cook up some pinto beans and have them available on the side for the uninformed who might want to add them, but never put them in the chili yourself!

Far be it for me to presume to give anyone writing tips, but here's what works for me: Set aside a time each day for writing and stick to the schedule. Write something even if you don't feel inspired. Once the juices are flowing, you never know what will come out.

Bill McGee's Award-Winning Chili

SERVES 6–8

In the 1950s, I left cowboyin' and turned in my Levis and boots for Brooks Brothers suits. I worked in the broadcasting field for thirty-two years and picked up this chili recipe from a television station client in San Antonio, Texas. Along the way, I made it my own and won several California and Texas chili cook-off contests. I like Hatch Medium Chile Powder from the Chile Shop, Santa Fe, New Mexico. If you want to reduce the heat, cut back on the cayenne, not the chile powder. This chili goes well with a cooling slaw such as . . . Sandra McGee's Southwest Slaw.

¼ cup olive oil

3 pounds chuck roast, cubed

1 quart water

9 tablespoons chili powder

3 teaspoons salt

1 teaspoon ground cumin

1 teaspoon dried oregano
   or dried marjoram

1 teaspoon cayenne

3 tablespoons paprika

6 tablespoons cornmeal
   mixed with 1 cup water
   for thickening

To anyone who has ever considered writing, there is only one way to do it— ass in chair.

Heat the olive oil in a 6-quart pot. When the oil is hot, add the cubed meat and sear it over high heat, stirring constantly until the meat is gray (not brown). The meat will have the consistency of whole-grain hominy. Add 1 quart of water, cover, and cook at a bubbling simmer for 1½ to 2 hours.

Add the spices and seasonings, and cook another 30 minutes at the same bubbling simmer. If much fat was left on the meat, it will rise to the top after the spices have been added. Skim off most of the fat before the cornmeal thickening is added.

Mix 6 tablespoons of cornmeal with 1 cup of water and add it to the chili. Simmer for 5 minutes to determine if more cornmeal or water is needed for the desired consistency. Stir the chili to prevent its sticking to the pot after the cornmeal is added.

Serving suggestions:
If you insist on beans, cook them separately, with no seasoning except salt.

If you wish for onions, serve them on the side. Never cook onions in the chili.

Nice accompaniments are cornbread, corn chips, saltine crackers, beer, and—surprise—milk.

Aileen Senior and Dawn Senior-Trask's Wyoming Chili

SERVES 4–6

I grew up in a log cabin without electricity or running water. My father was a writer and artist, and my mother was a genius at keeping the family warm, fed, and happy. She cooked on a wood range for years. When she was in her eighties, the Game and Fish Department gave her an antelope they had confiscated from a poacher, and she and I experimented until we came up with this delicious and filling way to use the ground game meat. I love it because I can work on my writing or other tasks between the simple cooking steps, and it can easily be adapted for ingredients I happen to have on hand. It makes enough for several meals for my small family.

Water, as needed

Brown the meat in a large stock pot over medium-high heat. Add the garlic and cook for a few minutes, but do not brown it.

Add the seasonings and blend well. Stir in the tomatoes and cook for 20 minutes.

Add the carrots and celery and cook for another 20 minutes.

Add the beans and cook for another 20 minutes.

Throughout the cooking process, add water as needed. Serve with rice.

2–3 slices pork or turkey bacon
1 pound ground game meat, beef, or turkey
2–3 cloves garlic, peeled and chopped
1 teaspoon salt
1 teaspoon brown sugar
1 teaspoon cumin
½–1 teaspoon chili powder
1 bay leaf
Pinch of oregano
Pinch of chives
Dash of Worcestershire sauce
1 (28-ounce) can stewed tomatoes, or fresh tomatoes (about 3½ cups)
1 cup carrots, chopped
1 cup celery, chopped
1 (15.5-ounce) can kidney beans
1 (15-ounce) can chili beans

Shoni Maulding's Meatless Chili
(aka Chili for When the City People Come to Visit)

SERVES 4

Yep, I was sorta a vegetarian for a few years when I was in my thirties. Horrified when looking back at that now, as I ate lots of cheese to substitute for beef. Sometimes I still like to make a pot of this chili for myself. And it works great on Indian tacos, too.

1 onion, chopped
1 clove garlic, chopped (or use garlic powder)
2 tablespoons oil
1 green pepper, diced
2 cups vegetable stock★
1 (15-ounce) can tomato sauce
1 cup whole kernel corn
4 cups kidney beans, cooked
1 teaspoon salt
½ teaspoon chili powder
¼ teaspoon cumin powder
1 teaspoon oregano

Sauté the onion and garlic in the oil in a large stockpot until the onion is soft. Add the green pepper and sauté another 2 to 3 minutes. Add the vegetable stock, tomato sauce, corn, beans, and seasonings. Cook over low heat for 30 minutes.

★If you are cooking the kidney beans from scratch, use the liquid from cooking them for your vegetable stock. If you are using canned kidney beans, do not rinse them but dump in the whole can. Add more tomato sauce and/or water if no veggie stock is available.

If you become involved with another person(s) in a book project, it is best to have a written contract beforehand. The involvement can grow immensely, and the time and information given out grows with it.

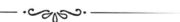

Robert Flynn's Stew for the Lion-Hearted

FEEDS 6 TREKKERS

Lions interrupted our safari camp stew dinner. We were told to go to our tents for safety. I knew that so many workers building the railroad from Nairobi to Mombasa were dragged out of tents by lions that the railroad hired hunters for protection. I slept fitfully hearing lions padding outside and drivers using the trucks to drive them away. At daybreak, I went to the campfire for coffee. There was no fire, no pot, no cooks, no drivers. They had slept in the trucks. Only we tourists spent the night in the tents! I asked Safari Chef Mbogo for the recipe for "Stew for the Lion-Hearted" and he obliged.

Place the meat and chicken broth in a Dutch oven and simmer until the meat is tender. Add the Ro-Tel and the liquid from the cans of green beans and corn. Add the onions, potatoes, and carrots and simmer until the vegetables are tender.

Add the beans, corn, Worcestershire sauce, black pepper, and Mrs. Dash. Stir the stew frequently and refrigerate it for 2 days. Heat it and serve it with cornbread.

2 pounds beef, lamb, warthog, or impala, chopped
2 (14–15-ounce) cans chicken broth
2 (10-ounce) cans Ro-Tel
1 (14–16-ounce) can green beans
1 (14–16-ounce) can whole kernel corn
Onions, as much as you like
Potatoes, as much as you like
Carrots, as much as you like
1 tablespoon Worcestershire sauce
Black pepper, to taste
Mrs. Dash (extra spicy), to taste

Ann McCord's Lawman Beef Stew, contributed by Monty McCord

SERVES 6 HUNGRY LAWMEN

Unable to find a homemade beef stew we liked, my wife created this winner. Don't let the list of ingredients scare you away from this Old West standby. What really sets this stew off is the addition of bacon! bacon! bacon! After using a rugged three-pronged fork, a good lawman and his deputies use hot buttered biscuits or a thick slice of sourdough bread to sop up this stew from their tin plates. It also makes great Dutch oven grub over your campfire next to a hot pot of coffee.

¼ cup flour
1½ teaspoons salt
¼ teaspoon pepper
2½ pounds beef stew meat, cut into bite-size pieces
1 tablespoon oil
3 slices bacon, finely diced
1 teaspoon garlic, minced
1 cup red wine
2 (14–15-ounce) cans beef broth (preferably reduced sodium and fat)
1 (8-ounce) can tomato sauce
1½ cups carrots, sliced
1 rib celery, finely diced
1 yellow onion, coarsely chopped
6–8 small red and/or Yukon Gold potatoes, cut into bite-size pieces
1 teaspoon sugar
2 bay leaves
½ teaspoon thyme
½ teaspoon sage
2–3 teaspoons Worcestershire sauce
4–6 dashes hot sauce (You'll like it—trust me!)

Combine the flour, salt, and pepper. Coat the beef pieces in the flour mixture.

Heat the oil in a 6-quart Dutch oven over medium heat. Add the bacon pieces and sauté them until the bacon begins to brown. Add the beef in small batches and sauté it in the bacon drippings until it is browned.

Add the garlic and sauté it for 1 minute. Add the red wine and scrape up the browned bits from the bottom of the Dutch oven.

Stir in the broth, tomato sauce, vegetables, and seasonings. Don't omit the hot sauce. It's just enough to kick up the flavor a bit, but not enough to make it spicy. Of course, if you like it spicy, feel free to add more!

Bring the stew to a boil. Reduce the heat and let it simmer, stirring occasionally, until the vegetables and meat are tender and the gravy is thickened. The flavor is best if it simmers for a couple of hours.

I don't believe in "writer's block," which is a self-imposed defeatist perspective. I find that a work slowdown or stoppage is due to lack of preparation and research.

Emil Franzi's Tortolita Eggplant

SERVES 6–8 COWHANDS OR 4 PUDGY ITALIANS

The Tortolita Mountains are on the border between Pima and Pinal Counties, in Arizona. While not as imposing as some other ranges, they are equally interesting. They held a wild horse herd until recent times, and sightings are still reported but may have other sources. The area around Twin Owl Peaks, towards the east or Oro Valley side, was the last home of famed Indian scout and Cochise negotiator Tom Jeffords, who both resided and mined there until his death in 1914. You can reach it only from the back side, off of I-10 in Pinal; these little hills are tougher than they look. I lived within sight of those peaks for thirty years before finding out the Jeffords connection. And both eggplant and zucchini grow well up here.

2 tablespoons olive oil

1 (11-ounce) can Campbell's condensed tomato soup

Generous sprinkling of dried basil leaves, or if available, fresh basil

6 large garlic cloves, chopped (Add more garlic if you're Italian!)

1 teaspoon salt

1 teaspoon sugar

2 large eggplants, cut into about ⅓-inch slices

2 large red onions, cut into about ¼-inch slices

5 large zucchini, cut into about ⅓-inch slices

8 ounces mozzarella, sliced or shredded

8 ounces provolone, sliced or shredded

4 ounces red wine or sherry

1 (14- or 16-ounce) jar or can high-quality tomato sauce (or make your own)

4–6 ounces Parmesan cheese, grated

Preheat the oven to 350°F. Coat the sides and bottom of a 12-inch Dutch oven with the olive oil.

Spread the tomato soup over the bottom, but do not mix. Sprinkle generously with the basil leaves and garlic. Sprinkle the salt and sugar evenly on top.

Build a series of layers as follows: eggplant, red onion, and zucchini. Add a layer of the cheese on top of the vegetable layers. (I suggest you alternate the provolone and mozzarella.) Build the layers all the way to the top of the Dutch oven—about 4 to 6 layers, depending on your cutting accuracy.

Drizzle the wine on top, then spread the tomato sauce and sprinkle with the Parmesan. Sprinkle more basil on that, and feel free to add more chopped garlic.

Bake for 75 to 90 minutes. Check it after 60 minutes for doneness.

Sandy Whiting's Tuna and Cheese Muffins

MAKES 12 MUFFINS

Ever wonder where the elusive tuna lives? I always thought it lived in the sea. But, apparently not. I have it on good authority that tuna resides on the shelves of grocery stores across the country. It is hidden in small tin cans and of late, can also be found in foil-lined flat packages touting the latest great catch of the day. Never one to shirk a good hunt, I can often be found "fishing" at a local store, hook, line, and sinker in hand. When caught, the "fun" catches can be turned into an excellent dinner selection. Add a few green veggies, fresh fruit, a hot roll or two, and voila! A complete meal is soon ready.

2 tablespoons minced fresh onion

1 tablespoon butter

2 cups white rice, cooked

1 cup sharp cheddar cheese, shredded

1–2 (5-ounce) cans tuna, drained

1 cup black olives, minced

1 teaspoon salt

2 tablespoons milk

2 eggs

Extra butter, melted and as desired

Parsley, fresh or dried

Preheat the oven to 375°F.

Sauté the onion in the butter until tender and set aside. Combine the white rice, cheese, tuna, olives, salt, milk, and eggs. Stir in the sautéed onions.

Divide the mixture into 12 muffin cups. Bake the muffins for 20 minutes. Garnish them with the extra butter and parsley.

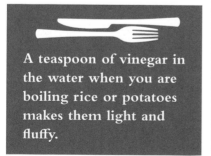

A teaspoon of vinegar in the water when you are boiling rice or potatoes makes them light and fluffy.

Ann Noble's Barbequed Beef Ribs

SERVES 4

Here at the Cora Valley Angus Ranch, in Cora, Wyoming, I usually serve fifty for lunch every branding. My meal has become standard over the years and consists of barbequed beef ribs, baked beans, coleslaw, potato and onion casserole, cornbread and honey butter, and a table full of desserts. I always hope it doesn't rain, not only so the job of branding gets done, but because the workers can eat outside. I have enough to clean with all the dishes, and I'm always thankful when I don't have to clean all the chairs! Here's my recipe for barbequed beef ribs.

In a large roasting pan, submerge the beef ribs in water and boil them for several hours, until the meat is tender. After cooling, trim off the fat and remove the bones.

While the ribs are cooking, mix all the sauce ingredients together. Heat the sauce, place the rib meat in a casserole dish, and smother it with the warm sauce.

The above recipe makes a small portion of sauce, so double, triple, or quadruple—as needed!

1 pound beef ribs
1 (12-ounce) bottle red chile sauce
⅓ cup brown sugar
¼ cup steak sauce
¼ cup cider vinegar
1 teaspoon onion powder
¼ teaspoon red hot sauce

Red chile sauce stains plastic utensils, blender pitchers, and clothes—pretty much everything it covers, contacts, or spatters.

Tammy Hinton's Hocks and Beans

SERVES 6–8

Eating beans always reminds me of my childhood. When it got near payday and money was short, there was always a pot of beans and cornbread. Instead of warming them the next day as leftovers, Mom threw in some brown sugar and ketchup, and with a couple of hot dogs, it was a whole new dish.

4 fresh pork hocks
2 tablespoons salt
¼ teaspoon pepper
2 cloves garlic, crushed
1 bay leaf
3 cups dry navy beans
  (1½ 16-ounce packages)
4 whole cloves
1 pound small white onions,
  chopped, leave 1 whole
1 pound carrots, cut in
  chunks
2 tablespoons lemon juice

Pour 5 cups of water into an 8-quart saucepot set on high and heat the pork, salt, pepper, garlic, and bay leaf to boiling. Simmer for 1½ hours.

Meanwhile, rinse the beans in water. Put 9 to 10 cups of boiling water in a 4-quart saucepan over high heat and add the beans. Boil for 2 minutes. Remove the beans from the heat and let them sit for 1 hour.

Drain the liquid from the beans. Add the beans to the hocks mixture and simmer for 30 minutes.

Stick the cloves into the one onion that you left whole. Add to the pot all the onions and carrots. Heat the mixture to boiling again, then reduce the heat and simmer until the meat and vegetables are done. Add the lemon juice at the end. Pick out the hocks and remove the meat. Return this meat to the pot.

Carol Crigger's Turkey Tetrazzini

SERVES ABOUT 8

My dad was a meat-and-potatoes kind of man. Spaghetti? He recoiled in horror. Any kind of pasta was a treat we got only if he was away at suppertime, although he would—under protest—eat macaroni salad with shrimp. I wonder what he'd think of this recipe. I only know my family likes it enough to ask me to make it now and again. I've got to say they like it better since I began using smoked turkey, pesto, and fettuccine noodles instead of spaghetti and walnuts. I like it because it makes enough for a couple of meals.

Cook the celery, green pepper, and onion in butter until the vegetables are soft. Do not brown.

Add the milk, soup, pesto, salt and pepper, Worcestershire sauce, and cheese. Cook, stirring, until the cheese melts.

Stir in the turkey and fettuccine. At this point, if you're pressed for time, you can heat it through and serve it with a sprinkling of the Parmesan. Or, turn the ingredients into a shallow, greased 2½-quart casserole, sprinkle with the Parmesan and nuts, and bake at 350°F degrees for about 25 minutes.

★You can substitute diced ham for the turkey.

¾ cup diced celery
½ cup diced green pepper
¼ cup minced onion
⅓ cup butter
1 cup milk
1 (10-ounce) can cream of mushroom soup
⅓ cup pesto, or to taste
Salt and pepper, to taste
1 tablespoon Worcestershire sauce
1 cup cheddar or Jack (or a combination of the two) cheese, shredded
2 cups cooked turkey★ (I prefer smoked turkey breast in a medium-size dice.)
2 cups cooked fettuccine, cut into 2-inch pieces
½ cup finely grated Parmesan cheese
¼ cup walnuts, chopped

Candace Simar's Mama's Cabbage Meatloaf

SERVES 4–6

My mother, Olive Jensen, was a farm woman who cooked simple, but hearty, fare. Her secret was farm-raised beef, home-grown vegetables, and, of course, meat and potatoes at every meal. Her cabbage meatloaf is a company meal, beautiful in presentation, though simple to prepare. I still make it every fall when the garden is overflowing with fresh cabbage. You may notice that she uses onion powder instead of chopped onions. Her concession to onion powder was because of me, the middle kid with a picky appetite. Thanks, Mom, it still warms my heart to remember. Mama always served this dish with baked squash and mashed potatoes.

1½ pounds extra-lean
   ground beef
½ cup bread crumbs
1 egg
¼ cup half-and-half
1 green pepper, finely
   chopped
1 teaspoon onion powder
1 clove garlic, crushed
1 teaspoon dried basil
Salt and pepper, to taste
1 cabbage
1½ cups chicken broth

Preheat the oven to 350°F.

Mix the above ingredients, except the cabbage and chicken broth, together and set them aside.

Slice the bottom of the cabbage to make it flat. Hollow out the inside of the cabbage so it is large enough for the meat mixture to fit inside. (The meat mixture should be even with the top of the cabbage.)

Place the cabbage, with the meat mixture inside it, in an ovenproof dish. Add the chicken broth around the cabbage.

Cover the dish and bake for 1½ hours. Uncover for the last 15 minutes to allow browning.

Carefully remove the cabbage from the dish and place it on a serving platter. Allow it to rest for a few minutes. Slice it into individual servings.

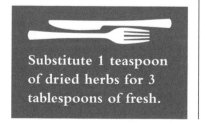

Substitute 1 teaspoon of dried herbs for 3 tablespoons of fresh.

While I'm in the middle of a writing project, I have a rule that I must work on it at least one minute a day. That means sitting in front of the computer screen with the manuscript in front of me; just thinking about it doesn't count. Why one minute? For me, the hardest part is forcing myself to start. Once I start working, I forget the clock. It works for me!

Linda and Richard Jacobs's Technicolor Dreams Lasagna

SERVES 6–8

A lot of lasagna is bland. Face it, Richard and I like things with a little kick to them, lots of basil and cinnamon and garlic and other spices guaranteed to give you Technicolor dreams. If you're afraid of nightmares, just dial back on the spices. We also added some Italian sausage for an extra boost. At our house, after the Thanksgiving turkey, we like to cook up a mess of what's known in our family as the traditional Christmas lasagna.

1 medium onion
1 red bell pepper
1 teaspoon olive oil
1 pound ground lamb
1 pound sweet Italian sausage
Red wine, to taste
1 (24-ounce) jar spaghetti sauce
12 cloves garlic
12 leaves fresh basil
1 teaspoon dried basil
1 teaspoon dried oregano
1 teaspoon cinnamon
1 teaspoon anise
1 teaspoon fennel
Salt, pepper, and extra garlic powder, to taste
12 precooked lasagna noodles
1 pound ricotta cheese
1½ pounds shredded mozzarella
½ pound shredded Italian 6-cheese blend

Preheat the oven to 350°F.

Dice the onion and red bell pepper. Sauté the onion in the olive oil, add the red bell pepper, and cook until soft.

Mix in the ground lamb and sweet Italian sausage, and cook until the meat is no longer pink. Add the red wine to taste and reduce down.

Add the spaghetti sauce and stir. Add all the spices after the spaghetti sauce and cook for 30 minutes until the flavors are appropriately mixed.

Layer the meat sauce, noodles, ricotta, and mozzarella cheese, repeatedly in that order. Top with the Italian 6-cheese blend.

Cover the lasagna with foil and bake for 45 minutes. Uncover it and cook 15 minutes more to brown the top. Allow the lasagna to rest for 10 more minutes and then serve.

Linda and Richard's Jacobs's Coq au Vin with More Wine

SERVES 4

I originally discovered coq au vin in the *Southern Living Cookbook*. Boy, do those folks know how to live! Almost every recipe starts with a quarter pound of butter. Our version starts with a quarter cup and is lighter, but it still has the rich flavor because we add extra wine and more and different spices. Amish roll butter, if you can find it, is really flavorful (I could eat it like cheese). We then simmer it down to a nice, thick sauce and serve it over our choice of rice. It's good with white rice, but a mix of wild and brown rice is our favorite. Bon appétit!

Cut the onion, bell pepper, and carrots into small pieces. Peel and finely chop the garlic cloves or smash them under the flat of a large chef's knife, then chop.

Put the coating ingredients in a gallon ziplock bag, add the chicken pieces, and shake and turn to coat.

In an electric skillet or large cast-iron skillet, melt the butter. Add the chicken and brown.

Add the red wine and onion, bell pepper, carrots, and garlic. Simmer covered, adding water periodically to thin the sauce, until chicken is tender and carrots are cooked through. Uncover and let the sauce thicken, watching carefully so it doesn't stick.

Serve coq au vin over a bed of rice, perhaps with a little more red wine in a goblet!

1 large onion
1 red bell pepper
4 medium carrots
5 cloves garlic
1 pound chicken, cut into small pieces
¼ cup butter (Amish roll butter or regular if you can't find it)
1 cup dry red wine
2 cups cooked white rice, or a mix of brown and wild rice

For the coating:
½ cup flour
½ teaspoon salt
½ teaspoon pepper
1 teaspoon parsley
½ teaspoon poultry seasoning
½ teaspoon tarragon
½ teaspoon savory

Rocío Nesbitt's Chile Colorado with Venison, contributed by John Nesbitt

SERVES 4–6

When my wife, Rocío, came to Wyoming from Chihuahua, Mexico, she brought a wealth of culture to share with me. My interests and hers are very compatible, as we raise our own garlic, chives, onions, chiles of various kinds, tomatoes, and more. I go out and hunt deer and antelope, and one of my favorite combinations of Wyoming and Mexican fare is this recipe. It is for chile colorado (the red chile) as it is made in northern Mexico. The sauce is used in enchiladas, as well as in other dishes. Rocío instructed me in the details of this recipe, and I have carried it out myself, as a way of sharing ownership of the recipe. The chile sauce is good for any other meat, of course, but for me, it is best for deer or antelope I have hunted myself. It gives a higher ratio of self-sufficiency in every bite.

15–20 dried red chiles, all of one kind or a mix, depending on what you have
1 tablespoon cooking oil, plus a couple of tablespoons more for frying the meat
2 tablespoons flour
2 teaspoons granulated garlic, plus more for flavoring the meat, if desired
1 teaspoon granulated or powdered onion
1 teaspoon cumin
1 teaspoon oregano
1 teaspoon dried chives
1 teaspoon salt, plus more for flavoring the meat, if desired
1 teaspoon pepper, plus more for flavoring the meat, if desired
Bit of parsley (optional)
2–3 pounds venison or other meat

Fill a 4- or 5-quart saucepan half-full of water, and put the water on to boil.

Wash the chiles, removing any dust, spoiled, or moldy bits. It is not necessary to remove the seeds at this point, but if some fall out it's okay.

Put the clean chile shells in the heating water. They will float, so it is necessary to weigh them down with something like a glass lid that is a size smaller than the one you are using. When the water comes back to a boil, lower the heat and let the chiles cook at a low boil for about 20 minutes.

When the chiles are soft, take them from the water and put them in a blender. Add 2 to 3 cups of water, either from the pan in which the chiles just boiled or from the tap. Sometimes the pan water has a bit of sand or other residue in the bottom, so some people prefer to use fresh water.

Place the clean pan on the stove, add a tablespoon of cooking oil. Sprinkle a tablespoon of flour in the pan

As for writing, learn to saddle your own horses. That goes for writing sentences and for knowing your subject matter at first hand.

and brown it. Put a second tablespoon of flour into the blender as well.

Add to the blender the granulated garlic and onion, cumin, oregano, chives, salt, and pepper. Some people use fresh garlic and onions, and some add a bit of parsley. Blend all of these ingredients with the chiles for about 3 minutes, until the mixture has an even consistency.

Using a strainer that fits into the pan, pour the mixture into the strainer and move the sludge around with a spoon so that the watery sauce will drain into the pan. Press the mash against the strainer as needed to squeeze the rest of the sauce into the pan.

Rinse the blender with about a cup of water, and pour that through the strainer as well, squeezing out the liquid. At this point, set the strainer and the leftover pulp aside.

Raise the heat until the sauce comes to a boil, then lower the heat and let the sauce simmer for about 15 minutes. Stir it occasionally and do not let it stick, as it will thicken at this time.

If you did not cut up the meat earlier, do so now. Cut it into pieces no larger than ¾ inch, and trim off any fat, tendons, or gristle. (You may also choose to use ground meat, which works fine as well.)

Pour a couple of tablespoons of cooking oil into a frying pan, and cook the meat at medium to high heat until it is brown on each side. Cooking the meat in an open pan helps get rid of some of the gamey flavor. You may choose to season the meat with salt, pepper, and garlic at this time, or you may choose to let the chile sauce do all the flavoring.

When the meat is cooked and the chile sauce is ready, combine the two and cook them together. If the meat is very tough, such as shank or some parts of the shoulder meat, you may want to cook the mixture in a slow cooker or Crock-Pot for a couple of hours. If the meat is not so tough, you may cook the mixture in the skillet you used for the meat; cook it at simmering heat for 20 to 30 minutes.

As observed earlier, this chile colorado sauce has a variety of applications. It is especially good for venison because it penetrates the meat and helps tenderize it. When the meat is cooked, you may roll it into burritos, mix it with beans, or serve it on a plate—however you like it best. And, of course, a cold bottle of Dos Equis or Negra Modelo goes well with this dish for some people. Buen provecho.

Amy Baker's Chicken 'n Dumplings, contributed by Julie and T. Lindsay Baker

SERVES 4–6

From the founding of the town in 1867 and continuing through the 1930s, it was common practice for residents of Cleburne, Texas, and all other communities in the American South to have henhouses and keep chicken runs in their backyards. This availability of fresh fowl allowed them the luxury of preparing a special Sunday lunch of chicken 'n dumplings. This recipe by Amy Baker was recorded by her grandson, T. Lindsay Baker, before her death in 1971.

1 chicken (live or prepared)
Cold water
1½ teaspoons salt, or to
    taste
¾ cup shortening
2 cups flour
1 egg
1 cup milk
2 tablespoons butter
½ teaspoon black pepper,
    freshly ground

Amy Baker was part of the generation that "discovered" pressure cookers, and she preferred to cook her stewing chickens using that specialized pan. If you follow her practice, place the prepared chicken and the desired internal organs into a pressure cooker with 2 or 3 cups of water, the amount depending on the size of the bird. Cook until the bird is done, about 10 to 12 minutes at the cooking pressure designated for your cooker, and slightly longer if your bird is old and tough. You want the bird to cook until it is tender.

Even though it takes longer, you can easily stew the chicken in a pot on top of the stove. Cut the chicken in half, add the desired internal organs, nearly cover it with water, bring the water to a boil, and then simmer the bird 20 to 30 minutes per pound, until it is tender. Add water as needed. Remember that if you are cooking an old bird, it will be tough and will require more cooking time, up to 3 or 4 hours. A tender, young bird will require only about 1½ hours.

After cooking the chicken, add 1 teaspoon of the salt, and slosh the bird around in the remaining broth to distribute the salt to all parts of the bird. Remove the body of the bird from the broth, saving the broth and internal organs and keeping them warm for use later in the preparation. Once the bird is cooked, cut it into pieces similar to those in a fried chicken—drumsticks, thighs, wings, breast, and back. Set aside but do not chill.

While the bird is cooking, begin preparing the dumplings. Amy Baker's dumplings retained substantial body, were made similarly to piecrust, and were not fluffy. Prepare the dough by cutting the shortening into the flour in a mixing bowl. Add a slight amount of salt, perhaps ¼ teaspoon, or to taste.

Cut the shortening into the flour the same way you would in making piecrust, making small "balls" of shortening about the size of green peas. Add the egg. Then gradually add small amounts of ice-cold water and mix it into a stiff dough about the same consistency as raw piecrust. Use your hands to shape the dough into a ball and place it onto a floured surface. Using a rolling pin, flatten the dough to about ⅜ inch thick. Then use a knife to cut the dough into strips about 1½ inches wide by about 6 to 8 inches long. Put the dough aside while you finish preparing the broth.

Having kept the chicken broth hot (with the pan on low), add the milk, butter, and black pepper. Bring the liquid to a gentle bubbling (not rolling) boil over medium heat.

Drop the strips of dumpling dough into the boiling broth, one after the other. Push them into the liquid if they "try" to float, keeping them from sticking together. Keep adding dumplings until all of them are immersed in the hot broth. Allow the dumplings to cook about 3 to 5 minutes. Do not stir the dumplings around too much. Just poke them down into the liquid and let them cook, or they will tear up as they soften.

When the dumplings are done, pour the dumplings and broth over the cut-up pieces of cooked chicken in a large serving bowl. Serve chicken 'n dumplings hot, and you will have re-created the Sunday dinner that graced the tables of Cleburne homes for decades.

Clay Reynolds's Grilled Chicken

SERVES 4

One of the problems people have with grilled chicken is how to cook it so it doesn't look like a charcoal briquette coated with burned ketchup. Grilling chicken requires attention and time, but it's not that hard. And a good deal of waiting can be passed by beer drinking, if it's done right. I mostly cook chicken thighs, as dark meat is juicy and flavorful. But for dinner guests, I use split breasts to satisfy their illusion that they're eating healthy.

You'll notice that no barbeque sauce is used. If you want the flavor of barbeque sauce, then heat it on the stove and brush it on the chicken when it's done. I use a marinade and use a variety depending on what I'm in the mood for. When I'm feeling lazy, I just use apple cider, orange juice, Italian salad dressing, or some wine. I've also used beer, Dr. Pepper, or Coca-Cola. Virtually any marinade that has an acid content will do.

8 chicken thighs
2 cups marinade, more or less

For the rub:
1 stick butter
½ teaspoon paprika
½ teaspoon salt
½ teaspoon black pepper
½ teaspoon garlic powder
½ teaspoon oregano
½ teaspoon cumin
¼ teaspoon cayenne
Dash of Tabasco
1 jalapeño pepper, seeded
    and chopped very fine
1 tablespoon honey
1 tablespoon white
    Worcestershire sauce
1 tablespoon lemon juice
2 teaspoons brown sugar

Place the chicken in a glass container and pour in enough marinade to completely cover the chicken. Usually, it's best to do this for several hours, even overnight.

Melt the butter and put it into a bowl. Add the remaining rub ingredients and stir until all the granular ingredients have dissolved.

Preheat the grill. Charcoal works best with this recipe. The coals should be cool enough to place your hand over the grill for a long count of three.

Place the chicken pieces on the grill, unadorned except for a spritz of olive oil and a light dusting of salt and pepper. Leave it on the grill for 10 minutes. Turn the pieces, then lightly brush on the prepared rub. If it drips onto the fire below, it'll flame up and burn your meat. Leave for 10 minutes and drink a beer.

Turn and brush the pieces again. Repeat this every 10 minutes for 1 hour. That's 6 full turns.

Remove the chicken from the grill. Allow it to rest for 10 minutes under a loose covering of foil. Serve.

Dennis McCown's Chile Rice Verde

SERVES 4–6

I first moved to Texas in the winter of 1973. At that time, my dad—in Wyoming—enjoyed canned tamales once in a while, but they were too spicy for me. Within a few years in Texas, however, I was eating and cooking Mexican food! It remains my favorite cuisine today.

Preheat the oven to 350°F.

Sauté the green chiles. (Hatch chiles in season are excellent! A 4-ounce can of green chiles can be substituted.) Combine the sour cream and chiles in a bowl and add salt to taste.

Place the rice in a buttered 1½-quart casserole dish. Top with the sour cream and chile mixture and then the Monterey Jack cheese.

Bake for 25 minutes. Remove the casserole from the oven and sprinkle it with the Parmesan cheese. Return it to the oven and bake for 5 minutes, or until the cheese is melted.

6 ounces green chiles, chopped
1 pint sour cream
Salt, to taste
Butter to grease the bottom of a casserole dish
3 cups cooked rice
½ pound Monterey Jack cheese, cut into strips
¼ cup grated Parmesan cheese

Dennis McCown's Smoked Beef Tenderloin

SERVES 4–6

For over twenty years, I was a weekend cowpoke, often involved in cattle gatherings in south Texas. Hundreds of angry two-year-old cows and steers kicking and pushing in narrow cattle chutes, and dusty cowpokes—not the ones on the beautiful horses and fancy saddles that gathered the cattle as a privilege, not the ones with the pressed denim shirts, not the ones with the thousand-dollar boots and fifty-thousand-dollar dually pickups—nope I was a cowpoke, stick or electric prod in hand, working the gates, shoving the cows, punching when I had to. My reward afterward was often an outstanding meal of smoked beef tenderloin cooked over an expansive mesquite fire, fire-baked potatoes, steamed green beans, and Dutch-oven fruit cobbler, perhaps served with homemade ice cream made with Fredericksburg peaches. Those were the days . . . !

2- to 3-pound beef
  tenderloin
½ cup Worcestershire sauce
Garlic salt, to taste
Cracked black pepper, to
  taste

If the tenderloin is not peeled (white skin removed), do so with a sharp knife. Coat the meat with the Worcestershire sauce, salt, and pepper. Marinate the meat for 2 hours at room temperature.

Prepare an outdoor smoker or grill. Establish a medium heat, but plan to cook slowly, off to the side.

Place the meat in the smoker or grill and cook until the internal temperature is 160°F, or medium-rare. Put the tenderloin aside for 20 minutes to allow the meat to rest and the juices to relax. It will continue cooking. Slice and serve.

Dennis McCown's Sweet & Sour Venison

SERVES 4–8

I learned to cook overseas—out of necessity—but cooking with joy came from a guy who cooked in Dutch ovens over an enormous, 15-foot-wide mesquite fire for roundup cowboys. I did it twice a year, at gatherings, and it was fun and good. I try to be fun and good, myself!

Flour the venison cubes and brown them in the butter. Add the boiling water and simmer for 30 minutes.

Meanwhile, boil the chile peppers in a separate pot until tender, about 25 minutes, and drain them.

Add the peppers and pineapple to the browned meat. Add the Sweet & Sour Sauce and some salt, to taste, and simmer for 10 minutes.

Serve over rice, chow mein noodles, or pasta.

½ pound flour
2 pounds venison, cut into 1-inch cubes
¼ cup butter
½ cup water, boiling
3 green chile peppers, cubed
½ cup diced pineapple chunks, fresh or canned
1 (8-ounce) package Sweet & Sour Sauce mix
Salt, to taste

Hank Corless's Snake River Sausage and Peppers

SERVES 4–6 HUNGRY RANCH HANDS

I have been making this skillet meal for years, as it cuts down on pots and pans and leaves more time for writing. Cleanup couldn't be easier. You can adapt this easy recipe to your own style of cooking. A little red pepper will make it hotter, for instance. Some people, mostly city folks, prefer to sauté the veggies in white wine. It works, but I prefer to keep it simple. PS: Don't tell anyone, but I use Italian sausage, and it works pretty darn good.

1 tablespoon vegetable oil
1½ pounds beef or pork
  sausages
1 red bell pepper
1 green bell pepper
1 yellow onion
1 bunch green onions
3 stalks celery
1 tablespoon butter
3 cloves garlic, minced
1 teaspoon sage
1 teaspoon basil
1 teaspoon ground black
  pepper

Heat the oil in a skillet over medium heat and add the sausages. Cover and cook for 5 minutes, turning a few times until brown. Remove and slice sausages into bite-size chunks.

Slice the two bell peppers lengthwise into ½-inch strips. Do the same with the yellow onion, but first cut it in half crosswise before cutting it into ½-inch strips. Chop up the green onions and celery into ½-inch lengths.

Melt the butter in the skillet and toss in the peppers, yellow onion, celery, garlic, sage, basil, and black pepper. Cover this and cook for 10 minutes, turning occasionally. Once they are tender, add the sausage and chopped green onions, and turn down the heat to simmer for another 8 to 10 minutes.

Toast up some garlic bread for a great feast!

Hank Corless's Porcupine Balls, Thunder Mountain Style

SERVES 4–6 HUNGRY RANCH HANDS

I came across the basic recipe for this dish about thirty years ago. I was digging through the cupboards trying to find something that would be fast, cheap, and would feed some unexpected guests who had stopped by. Since then I have tinkered with the ingredients a little, and what you see here is my favorite mix. The addition of the sauce or just the ketchup on the side can add even more flavor. Serve it with mashed potatoes and garlic bread, and the cowhands will think you are a real mountain chef.

Combine the diced bell pepper and jalapeños with the Rice-A-Roni rice-vermicelli mix (but not the Special Seasonings), ground beef, and egg. Shape this mixture into 6 tennis-ball-size meatballs. In a large skillet, heat the oil over medium-high heat and add the meatballs, carefully turning them to brown on all sides.

Slowly pour the stewed tomatoes over the meatballs. Add the water, mixed with the Special Seasonings from the Rice-A-Roni package. Bring this to a boil. Cover, reduce the heat to low, and simmer for 20 to 30 minutes, or until the meatballs are cooked. Uncover for the final 5 minutes of cooking time to allow most of the liquid to escape.

Make up a side dish with the ketchup and Heinz 57 Sauce for those who would like to add a tangy flavor.

1 green bell pepper, diced into ¼-inch chunks
2 jalapeño peppers, diced into ¼-inch chunks
1 box Rice-A-Roni Beef Flavor
1 pound ground beef
1 egg
1 tablespoon vegetable oil
1 (16-ounce) can stewed tomatoes
2 cups water
½ cup ketchup
½ cup Heinz 57 Sauce

Thom Nicholson's Chiles Rellenos

SERVES 8

This is a recipe that my mother developed during the time we lived in New Mexico, during the 1950s.

1 (27-ounce) can whole green chiles
1 pound cheddar cheese, sliced or shredded
1 pound Monterey Jack cheese, sliced or shredded
4 eggs
1 (12-ounce) can evaporated milk
3 tablespoons flour
Salt and pepper, to taste
2 (14.5-ounce) cans tomato sauce
Hot sauce (optional)

Preheat the oven to 325°F.

Remove the seeds and flatten half of the chiles on the bottom of a 9 x 13-inch casserole pan.

Cover the chiles with a layer of the cheddar cheese. Put the rest of the chiles on top of the cheese.

Add a layer of the Monterey Jack cheese.

Separate the egg whites and yolks into separate bowls. Beat the egg whites and set aside.

Beat the yolks and then add the milk and flour, plus the salt and pepper. Fold in the beaten egg whites and pour this mixture on top of the cheese layer.

Cover the pan loosely and bake for 1 hour. Then pour the tomato sauce over the top and bake an additional 30 minutes, uncovered. Add hot sauce if you wish this dish to be hotter. Tastes great!

Rocky Gibbons's Montana Moose Skillet

SERVES 4

I came up with this recipe years ago, when my husband and I lived in Montana near the Canadian border. He had harvested a moose that year, and I had to come up with all kinds of inventive recipes to use up all of that delicious meat!

Brown the meat and onion in a pan. Drain off the fat and add the rest of the ingredients, except for the cheese and crushed tortilla chips. Cover the pan and simmer, stirring occasionally, for 20 minutes.

Before serving, top Montana Moose Skillet with the cheese and chips.

1 pound ground moose (or beef, elk, or venison)
¾ cup chopped onion
½ teaspoon garlic salt
½ teaspoon salt
1½ teaspoons chili powder
¾ cup water
¾ cup instant rice
1 (16-ounce) can whole tomatoes
1 (15-ounce) can red kidney beans
3 tablespoons green peppers, chopped
Cheddar cheese, shredded
Tortilla chips, crushed

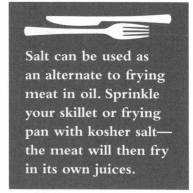

Salt can be used as an alternate to frying meat in oil. Sprinkle your skillet or frying pan with kosher salt—the meat will then fry in its own juices.

Jennifer Smith-Mayo and Matthew Mayo's Team Gritty Dutch Oven Chicken

SERVES 4 WELL-RESTED CAMPERS (OR 2 RAVENOUS HIKERS!)

A few years ago, we of Team Gritty (aka award-winning photographer and videographer Jennifer Smith-Mayo and Spur Award–winning author Matthew P. Mayo) sold our home in Maine and took to the road, running Gritty Press (www.GrittyPress.com) and traveling all over the US map in search of hot coffee, tasty whiskey, and high adventure. Not surprisingly, we spend most of our time roving the West, writing and researching books, hiking, photographing, and, our favorite activity—enjoying campfires. The Dutch oven has long been a favorite mode of cooking for us, and Jennifer's recipe for Team Gritty Dutch Oven Chicken remains a staple, no matter where we go! Serve it with a side of Dutch oven biscuits . . . and enjoy!

1 whole chicken (with backbone and organs removed), cut into pieces (Our 10-inch oven fits a small chicken cut into 6–8 pieces: 2 breasts, 2 thigh/drumstick combos, 2 wings.)

1–2 cups chicken or vegetable stock

12–15 fingerling or small red potatoes, washed, and, if large, cut into chunks

2 carrots, cleaned and cut into quartered small sticks or short rounds

2 small onions, peeled and cut into quarters

2–3 cloves garlic, peeled (optional)

4–5 sprigs fresh thyme

2 good-size sprigs fresh rosemary

3–4 fresh sage leaves

Black pepper, freshly ground, to taste

Pinch of sea salt

½ cup (or more) vermouth or white wine

Write standing up! It keeps you on your toes. And take frequent perambulations—good for your body, good for your book, and good for your brain.

Rinse the chicken pieces and pat them dry with paper towels.

Pour the stock in the bottom of a Dutch oven (it should be about ¼ inch deep). Arrange the chicken pieces along the bottom. Layer the potatoes on top of the chicken. Next, layer the carrots, onions, and garlic cloves. Lay the fresh herbs over the carrots.

Grind the black pepper over the pot and add a pinch of sea salt. Splash about ½ cup of vermouth or white wine over everything. Cover the Dutch oven with its lid.

To cook the chicken outdoors with charcoal:
Prepare about 24 to 30 charcoal briquettes with a charcoal starter (the number of briquettes used depends on the size of your oven). When the briquettes are glowing whitish-gray and are good and hot, lay about 12 to 14 of them to make a rough, filled-in circle on the bottom of your fire pit, then place your Dutch oven over the briquettes. (Our 10-inch Dutch oven doesn't have feet so we place a collapsible stand down first, lay the briquettes in and around the stand, then set our oven on top of the stand.) Then place 14 to 16 briquettes on the top of the lid.

Cook for 30 to 45 minutes, possibly longer depending on the size of your chicken pieces. Check every 15 to 20 minutes to make sure everything looks good (careful, it'll be steaming when you open the lid) and the briquettes are still in good shape. If you're cooking outdoors in winter, as we frequently do, midway through you'll probably need to refresh the briquettes with another batch of hot ones. The chicken is cooked through when you poke it in the thickest part with a knife or fork and the juices run clear; potatoes and carrots are done when easily pierced with a fork.

To bake the chicken in the kitchen oven:
Preheat the oven to 375°F. Place the covered Dutch oven in the oven and bake for 30 to 45 minutes. Check at 25 to 30 minutes. Same as above, the chicken is cooked through when you poke it in the thickest part with a knife or fork and the juices run clear; potatoes and carrots are done when easily pierced with a fork.

Melissa Elsmo's Fry Bread Stacks, contributed by Paul Colt

SERVES 4–6

This is a recipe my daughter Melissa Elsmo created for the Western Writers of America cookbook. She's a professional chef, writer, photographer, and food editor for the *Chicago Tribune*. I asked her to do something "Western" for us. She starts with a Navajo fry bread . . . and finishes with wow. This may not have been daily fare in your average hogan, but it is sure to treat the taste buds of any Western foodie. It's a long list, but stick with it!

For the slow-cooked pork:
¼ cup canola oil
1 4-pound pork shoulder roast
Salt and pepper, to taste
2 sweet onions, thinly sliced
6 cloves garlic, smashed
1 jalapeño, quartered and seeded
1 teaspoon cumin
½ teaspoon turmeric
1 cup apple juice
⅔ cup unfiltered apple cider vinegar
1 (14-ounce) can reduced sodium chicken broth

For the colorful bean compote:
2 ears sweet corn, shucked
1 tablespoon sugar (optional)
1 cup pinto beans, cooked, rinsed and drained
1 cup dark red kidney beans, cooked, rinsed and drained
1 cup halved grape tomatoes

1 red pepper, chopped
½ cup chopped cilantro
1 bunch scallions, sliced
1 jalapeño, seeded and minced (optional)
½ cup fresh lime juice
¼ cup olive oil
Salt and pepper, to taste

For the fry bread foundation:
2½ cups flour, plus more for dusting a rolling pin and cutting board
1 tablespoon baking powder
½ teaspoon chili powder
1 teaspoon salt
1–1½ cups cold water
Oil or shortening for frying

For serving:
2 avocados, mashed
Scallions, sour cream, hot sauce, and cheese, if desired

To prepare the pork:

Heat the canola oil in a large Dutch oven over high heat until it is hot, but not smoking. Season the pork liberally with salt and pepper, and sear it on all sides until it is a deep golden brown (about 6 minutes per side). Transfer the browned meat to a sheet tray.

Add the onions to the pot and reduce the heat to medium. Season the onions with salt and pepper, and allow them to cook, stirring frequently until they are soft and golden brown (about 10 minutes). Add the garlic, jalapeño, cumin, and turmeric, and cook until they are just fragrant (about 45 seconds).

Add the apple juice, cider vinegar, and chicken broth to the pot. Stir it well and return the pork to the mixture (the liquid should come halfway up the sides of the meat). Bring this to a boil, reduce the heat, and cover the pot tightly.

Place the pot into a 300°F oven for 3 hours, or until the meat shreds easily with a fork. Keep it warm until the stacks are ready to be assembled.

To prepare the bean compote:

Place the corn in a pot of cold water and add the sugar, if desired. Bring this to a boil, cover the pot, and remove it from the heat. Allow the corn to stand in the water for 15 minutes before removing it and allowing it to cool.

Using a sharp knife, cut the kernels away from the cob and scoop them into a mixing bowl. Add the beans, tomatoes, pepper, cilantro, scallions, and jalapeño to the corn, and mix everything well.

Whisk the lime juice and olive oil together and season with salt and pepper. Toss the dressing with the bean mixture and set this aside until the stacks are ready to be assembled.

To prepare the fry bread:

Combine the dry ingredients in a large mixing bowl. Gradually add the water and mix gently until a soft dough forms. Do not overwork the dough. Allow the dough to rest in a covered bowl for 30 minutes.

Divide the dough into 6 to 8 balls. Dust a rolling pin and cutting board with flour, and roll each dough ball into an oval ¼ inch thick.

Heat the oil until it is hot, but not smoking, and fry the bread in batches until it is golden brown and crispy on both sides (about 2 to 3 minutes per side). Drain the bread on paper towels.

To assemble the dish:

Place a piece of fry bread on each plate. Top it with a portion of the pork and a generous helping of the bean compote. Garnish this as desired, and serve it at once.

Bill Groneman's Dueling Meatballs

SERVES 3–10, DEPENDING ON THE VERSION

My mom, Jean Novak, and I created this recipe. The traditional version is old-style Italian Brooklyn all the way. The alternate version is more Western. The combination of beef and lamb evokes the idea of cattlemen and dang sheepherders. Meatballs, regardless of the recipe, can stand as a meal on their own. You are not an Italian from New York City if you have never been met at the door by your mother holding a meatball on a fork for you. Meatballs are great as leftovers, so don't be afraid to make a gang of them. They are especially good as leftovers on a couple pieces of toast, with sauce and grated cheese, eaten with a knife and fork.

Version One: Bill's Mom's Traditional Meatballs

5 slices white bread
3 pounds chuck chopped
    beef or ground round
Salt and pepper, to taste
1 teaspoon sugar
5 tablespoons grated
    Locatelli or Romano
    cheese
2 eggs
1 Titleist golf ball
Canola oil

Grate or crumble 5 slices of bread (remove the top brown crust first) in a large bowl.

Add the meat, and shake in a little salt and pepper. Add the sugar, grated cheese, and eggs (without the shells). Mix it all by hand.

Shape the meatballs a little bigger than a golf ball (this is where the Titleist comes in for sizing).

Coat a frying pan with a little oil and fry the meatballs on medium heat, turning them over once or twice so they brown evenly.

This recipe should yield about 30 (yes, 30) meatballs. Serve them plain or in your favorite sauce (gravy in Italian households), as an appetizer or as a side dish. They can be served in the classic way with macaroni (pasta in yuppie households) and sauce. Bada-bing! Mangia!

Version Two: Bill's Alternative Meatballs

Put the meat and bread crumbs in a large bowl. Shake in a little Parmesan cheese, the pepper, and the sugar. Add a dash of Worcestershire sauce and the Marsala wine and mix it all by hand. At this point you have to decide whether to bake the meatballs in the oven or grill them.

If you decide to bake: Place the meatballs on a baking sheet or glass pan that is either sprayed with oil or lined with foil, and bake at 350°F. Monitor and turn the meatballs from time to time until they are done enough to your liking.

If you decide to grill: Make sure you've made the meatballs big enough so they don't fall through the grill. Fire up the grill. Grill the meatballs as you would hamburgers, turning frequently.

The recipe should yield about 9 meatballs. Serve them as suggested above, in the traditional recipe.

½ pound ground beef (the leanest you can find)
½ pound ground lamb
Bread crumbs (Italian style or regular)
Parmesan cheese (The fake kind in the round plastic containers is OK. If anyone asks, just shrug your shoulders dismissively and say, "Ay, I don't know from nothin'!")
Ground black pepper, to taste
1 tablespoon sugar
Worcestershire sauce
Marsala cooking wine

Bill Groneman's Seafood al Grono

SERVES 2

I like this recipe because I invented it myself. It doesn't take long to prepare, and it is very tasty using simple ingredients. And, you get to throw out the tinfoil vessel, so that is one less thing you have to wash. You can vary ingredients without changing the recipe too much. For example, you can use this over some other type of pasta or over white rice. If you want to make the recipe more Western, wear a cowboy hat while cooking. Enjoy!

1 pint Jameson's Irish whiskey
1 or 2 cans Guinness Irish stout beer
6 jumbo shrimp
3 large sea scallops
Chunky Salsa or Picante Sauce (mild), or any other salsa you prefer
Butter
Garlic, chopped
2–3 lemons
Olive oil
Thin spaghetti
Parmesan cheese

Take a nip of Jameson's, munch it thoughtfully, and follow up with a sip of Guinness. Ahh! You are now ready to begin.

Fire up the grill.

Take a piece of heavy-duty tinfoil, maybe 9 x 12 inches or so, and turn up the sides so it resembles a sort of boat. Make sure you don't puncture the foil, and crimp the edges so it doesn't leak. Keep the bottom flat. Do this on a fairly large plate so it is easier to carry.

Peel, clean, and devein the shrimp. Clean the scallops and cut them into halves or quarters.

Place the shrimp and scallops in the tinfoil vessel. Pour some of the chunky salsa or picante sauce over the shrimp and scallops. Judge for yourself as to how much.

Put in a couple of spoonfuls of butter. Once again, how much is up to you. Add some chopped garlic to the mix. (Let's be honest. Why knock yourself out chopping garlic when one of those little squat jars with chopped garlic floating in olive oil is perfectly good? You don't have to tell anyone.)

Squeeze 2 or 3 lemons over the top. It's OK to leave some of the lemon pulp in, but make sure you get all the seeds out. (Hey, if you didn't want to chop the garlic, you probably don't want to squeeze lemons. If you use one of those little plastic fake lemons with lemon juice in it, your secret is safe with me.)

When the grill is ready, place the tinfoil vessel on the grill, being especially careful not to puncture it. While the seafood is cooking, set a pot of water with a little olive oil in it to boil. Check in with Mr. Jameson and Mr. Guinness to make sure everything is going OK.

Every now and then, stir the seafood on the grill carefully with a large silicon or plastic spoon. Place the thin spaghetti in the pot once the water is boiling. You judge how much. When done to your liking, drain the spaghetti.

Remove the tinfoil vessel from the grill after the sauce in it boils and the shrimp get to a good pink color. It doesn't take too long. Don't overcook it! The best way to remove it is to place the whole vessel on a dinner bowl.

Serve the seafood over the spaghetti, making sure that all served get equal amounts of the shrimp and scallops. You don't want fights.

Sprinkle on some Parmesan cheese, but use the good stuff that you've grated yourself, not the kind in those plastic jars. Serve with a nice, light, spring mix salad or maybe some green peas over the spaghetti, or some sliced avocados around the edges of the plate or bowl.

Use the juice from the vessel as sauce. That is why you shouldn't scrimp on the ingredients. You're going to want that sauce and plenty of it.

Have a nice wine that goes with seafood. It is almost mandatory that you have something made out of chocolate after this.

Julie and T. Lindsay Baker's Farm Possum 'n Taters

SERVES 4–6

This recipe was created in the kitchen yard of Julie and T. Lindsay Baker on the J. T. Baker Farmstead, near Blum, Texas. Home-style possum 'n taters can be an old-time wintertime treat for your family. Through the combination of nineteenth-century remembrances and practical open-fire cooking trials, the Bakers have perfected the following directions for modern kitchen-yard chefs to re-create this popular and taste-tempting dish enjoyed by many of our ancestors. Its closest comparable taste in modern foods is baby back ribs. According to former Oklahoma slave Lizzie Farmer of Mount Enterprise, Texas, "When we cooked possum that was a feast. We would skin him and dress him and put him on top of the house and let him freeze for two days or nights. Then we'd boil him with red pepper, and take him out and put him in a pan and slice sweet 'taters and put round him and roast him. My, that was good eating."

1 adult but young opossum, killed in the depth of winter

1 large metal pot, at least 4 gallons in capacity

1 tablespoon salt

1 tablespoon ground red pepper

8 medium-size sweet potatoes, about 6 inches long and no more than 2 inches thick

2 onions

1 cup butter or lard

1 cast-iron Dutch oven with cast-iron lid, at least 12 inches in diameter

Plan to spend 3 to 4 hours preparing this meal, as you must allow time to parboil the possum until it is tender.

Start with one adult but young possum killed in "the season" during the depth of winter in January or February. (At this season the animals are less likely to have any objectionable parasites.) Disembowel, clean, and skin the possum, removing its feet and head. Wash the possum body in fresh water. (If you would prefer to cook the meal at a later time, it is easy to put the possum in a plastic bag and freeze it at this point.)

Place the possum in a large metal pot with about 3 gallons of water, the salt, and the ground red pepper, and bring this to a boil. Continue cooking the possum at a low boil, changing the water and pouring off the fat at least 3 times. Each time refill the pot with fresh water and seasonings. (A 4-gallon cast-iron "wash pot" on an open fire in the kitchen yard works perfectly at this stage of preparation. Take care that the fire does not spread.)

Continue to parboil the possum until it is tender. This may take as long as 2 or 3 hours, depending on the possum's age and toughness. Regularly changing the water removes the distinctive possum fat and any "game" taste.

Wash the sweet potatoes, leaving them in their skins. Set them aside for later use.

After the possum has become tender, remove it from the pot and allow it to cool slightly.

While the possum cools enough for you to handle it, peel and slice the onions. Place the onions in the Dutch oven with the butter and sauté them until they become transparent.

Cut up the cooked possum into 8 portions (4 legs and 4 quarters of its torso). Line the bottom of the Dutch oven with the sweet potatoes, still in their jackets, mixing them with the sautéed onions. Then add the possum pieces so that they are spread through the sweet potatoes in the vessel.

Place the lid on the Dutch oven, then move it to where you have spread on the ground 6 good-size coals from the fire and place the cooking vessel on top of the coals. Then with a shovel or tongs, place 6 more good-size coals from the fire on top of the lid. (Take care not to overheat the Dutch oven and thereby scorch your meal.) Allow the combined possum and taters to cook for about 45 minutes, or until the sweet potatoes have baked and the possum has browned.

Serve this dish hot to your appreciative family members.

Audrey Smith's World Steak, contributed by Brad Smith

SERVES 4

This recipe came about because there are no Chinese restaurants in the small local town we travel to for all amusements and shopping. We end up going to the big city of Tucson for international ingredients. We make our own Chinese food (rather my wife does; she is the great cook). This recipe is a combination of traditional Southwestern-style carne asada (grilled steak served on tortillas) with a hot Southeast Asian twist. We have enjoyed it for twenty-five years.

1 2-pound London broil
  steak
¼ cup vegetable oil
¼ cup unseasoned rice
  vinegar
3 tablespoons soy sauce
1 tablespoon minced garlic
Sriracha or other hot chile-
  based sauce, to taste

Place the steak in a nonreactive container and add the remaining ingredients to marinate it in. Soak overnight in the refrigerator, turning the roast halfway through the process.

Grill the meat as preferred. For a 1½-inch steak, we like medium-rare, grilled at a high heat for 6 minutes per side. Allow the meat to rest for 10 minutes, and then slice it thin across the grain.

Serve with taco-size flour tortillas, salsa, sour cream, and cilantro sprigs.

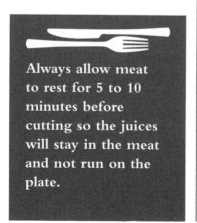

Always allow meat to rest for 5 to 10 minutes before cutting so the juices will stay in the meat and not run on the plate.

Chapter Five

End of the Trail (Desserts)

There aren't many writers who, at some point in deadline mode, haven't caved in to something sweet. Whether it's a healthy fruit, a candy bar, or something chocolate—we indulge. Some of us like our sweets more than others, and we have the recipes to prove it!

We writers appreciate a boost, and that often comes in the form of something deliciously sweet. Some of us firmly believe that dessert should be eaten any time of the day and is a welcome pick-me-up not only after dinner, but also with that morning cup of coffee or during that afternoon slump. It's all here in this chapter, from banana pudding and butter cake to Texas sheet cake and even homemade ice cream. These recipes are 100 percent guaranteed to help you on to the next paragraph.

Nancy Plain's Hot Fruit Casserole

SERVES 6

This is an old—and delicious—standby from my mother. She made it often for family dinners, and it is an easy side dish that you can assemble a day or two before serving. The recipe is flexible, too. If you don't like one of the fruit types listed below, just add another of your choice. Hot fruit bubbling in the oven makes your kitchen smell sweet!

3–4 apples, sliced

Sugar, to taste

Cinnamon, to taste

1 (15-ounce) can sliced peaches, drained

1 (20-ounce) can pineapple chunks, drained

1 (15–16 ounce) can pitted black cherries, drained

1–2 bananas, sliced and dipped in lemon juice

1 (12-ounce) can undiluted frozen orange juice

2 tablespoons cornstarch

Preheat the oven to 400°F.

Place the apple slices in a deep baking dish and sprinkle the sugar and cinnamon on top (but don't use too much of these). Over this, place the rest of the fruit in layers, ending with mingled banana slices and cherries.

In a separate bowl, combine the frozen orange juice and cornstarch, and pour this mixture over the fruit. Bake the fruit for 1 hour.

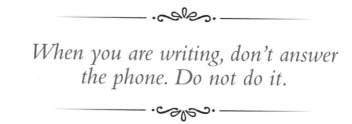

When you are writing, don't answer the phone. Do not do it.

Nancy Burgess's Scottish Shortbread

MAKES 8 WEDGES OR 12 SQUARES

I've found a number of shortbread recipes in magazines and cookbooks and tried them. Once I tasted shortbread at a bakery in Scotland, though, I wanted a simpler recipe of my own, as the traditional Scottish shortbread has only a few ingredients. I asked the baker what was in her recipe, and she told me "real butter, flour, sugar, and thickener." So I found a similar recipe and used the best-quality "real" butter and cornstarch as the "thickener." I experimented until I got the consistency and flavor that I remembered from the bakery in Scotland. I have made this recipe every Christmas for many years. These are quick and very easy cookies. They keep well and can be frozen.

Preheat the oven to 325°F.

Whisk the flour, sugar, and cornstarch together. Add the butter. Mix the dough with your hands until it makes crumbs, making sure that all of the butter is incorporated.

Dump the dough into an 8- or 9-inch square or round cake pan. Pat the dough into the pan until it is firm. Prick the dough all over with a cake tester or toothpick.

Bake for 30 to 40 minutes. The shortbread is done when the top begins to brown.

Remove the shortbread from the oven and sprinkle it with flavored, plain, or sanding sugar. Cut it into squares or wedges while it is still warm. Remove it from the pan when cooled.

1¼ cups all-purpose flour, unsifted
¼ cup sugar, plus extra for dusting the tops of the shortbread
3 tablespoons cornstarch
1 stick butter, cut into small chunks

Gail L. Jenner's Grandma Muzzy's Chocolate Cake

MAKES 12-LAYER CAKE

Grandma Muzzy's recipe for devil's food cake was (and still is) known to be unbelievably rich and good. Grandma would have used her own fresh eggs (she raised over one hundred chickens and turkeys), her own fresh milk, and her own fresh butter. The flour would have come from the nearby flour mill, which was adjacent to the Wagner Ranch.

1 cup sugar
1 cup dark chocolate chips
1 cup milk
½ cup butter
½ cup brown sugar
3 egg yolks, beaten
2 cups flour
½ teaspoon baking soda

Preheat the oven to 350°F.

Melt the sugar, chocolate chips, and milk together over low heat. Cool slightly.

Cream the butter and brown sugar, and add the beaten yolks.

Combine the flour and baking soda in a separate bowl.

Add the dry ingredients alternately with the melted mixture to the creamed mixture, blending well after each addition.

Pour the batter into two cake pans that have been greased and floured. Bake until the cake springs back to the touch, about 20 to 25 minutes.

Remove and cool slightly in pans for 10 minutes, then remove from pans and cool on racks.

Frost with Chocolate Frosting (next page) or a favorite frosting.

Chocolate Frosting

FROSTS 1 CAKE

Place the ingredients in a saucepan over low heat. Stir constantly until it's all blended and smooth. This will take about 10 minutes and will look like pudding. Cook until slightly thickened.

Frost cake immediately.

5 ounces dark chocolate

2 eggs, beaten

1 teaspoon cornstarch or flour

1 cup milk

¼–½ cup sugar, to taste

Invest in yourself and your career: Whether it's attending conferences, taking classes, buying materials—don't go cheap! You have to believe enough in yourself to spend money on developing your skills and learning about the world of publishing.

Bill Markley's Mom's Wet Bottom Shoofly Pie

MAKES 2 PIES

Being of Pennsylvania Dutch heritage and raised in Pennsylvania Dutch country, I grew up eating wonderful foods such as piccalilli, scrapple, Lebanon baloney, funny cake, and shoofly pie. Shoofly pie is a Pennsylvania Dutch—that is, German—breakfast cake. Cake or pie? That's a controversy in and of itself. But it's one of my favorite foods. I heard it's called "shoo fly" because when the pie was set on an open windowsill to cool in the breeze, flies would come buzzing around and would have to be shooed away. This recipe that my mom, Gloria Markley, used came from an old German cookbook.

2 single piecrusts
1 cup boiling water
1 rounded teaspoon baking
  soda
½ cup dark blackstrap
  molasses
½ cup Karo dark syrup
3½ cups flour
1 cup sugar
½ cup shortening
½ cup butter

Preheat the oven to 350°F. Line pie pans with the piecrusts.

For the filling, mix the boiling water, baking soda, molasses, and Karo syrup in a bowl.

In a separate bowl, mix the flour, sugar, shortening, and butter together to make the crumb topping.

Divide the the filling in half and pour into the pie crusts and put the crumbs on top. Bake for 45 minutes. Take the pies out of the oven. Eat.

Liz Markley's Chocolate Cake from Scratch, contributed by Bill Markley

MAKES 1 CAKE

I love chocolate. When selecting dessert, I usually go for whatever is made of chocolate. I'm one-dimensional—chocolate ice cream or chocolate milkshakes for me. Liz's chocolate cake is the best I have ever eaten. And it's not just me; when friends stop at the house and learn that Liz has made her chocolate cake, they beg for some. Not only is the cake itself good, but the icing can't be beat, and when joined together they create a mouthwatering extravaganza. Now that I've written this, I'll have to see if Liz is willing to make me one.

Preheat the oven to 350°F.

Mix all the ingredients, except the water, in a large bowl and blend. Add the boiling water and stir to combine.

Grease and flour a 9 x 13-inch pan and pour the batter into it. Bake for 35 to 40 minutes. Apply frosting (see below) to the cake. Eat.

2 cups sugar
½ cup cocoa
2½ cups flour
2 teaspoons baking soda
½ teaspoon salt
1 cup buttermilk
2 eggs
1 cup oil
1 teaspoon vanilla extract
1 cup boiling water

Frosting

Mix all the ingredients, except the chocolate chips, together in a saucepan. Cook over medium-high heat for 1 minute and bring to a boil. Remove from heat and stir in the chocolate chips until melted. Don't stir too much or it will get sugary.

1 cup sugar
¼ cup milk
¼ cup cocoa
¼ cup butter
½–¾ cup chocolate chips

Barbara Dan's Sweet Potato Pie

MAKES 1 PIE

I was sorely tempted to include my recipe for Rattlesnake Hors d'Oeuvres but figured that processing the main ingredient might lead to mishaps in the wrong hands and to unintentional liability! In fact, I was going to include this recipe in my latest historical Western romance, *Home Is Where the Heart Is*, but decided at the last minute it would be safer to delete it. Since I deleted it from the book, I decided to submit it for the WWA cookbook. Cheers!

3 medium-size sweet
  potatoes
¼ cup butter, room
  temperature
2 eggs, separated
½ cup strained honey
¼ teaspoon salt
¼ teaspoon nutmeg
1 teaspoon baking powder
1 cup milk
½ teaspoon grated orange
  rind, packed
1 teaspoon brandy extract
3 tablespoons sugar
Pastry for 9-inch single
  crust

Adjust oven rack to 4 or 5 inches from the bottom of oven. Preheat the oven to 450°F.

If not using a readymade piecrust from the store, roll out the pastry dough and place in a 9-inch pie pan. Trim off the edges with scissors ½ inch beyond the pan rim, then turn the overhang under so it's even with rim. Crimp the edge with a fork or flute with your finger. Do not prick crust. Cover the pastry-lined pan with waxed paper.

Scrub the sweet potatoes thoroughly in cold water, place in a 3-quart saucepan, and cover with hot water. Heat to boiling, then reduce heat to a gentle boil, cover the pan, and cook the potatoes until soft, about 20 to 25 minutes. Drain the potatoes, skin while hot, and rub them through a food mill or sieve to remove fibers. Cool slightly.

Beat in the butter, then the egg yolks, honey, salt, nutmeg, and baking powder, until smooth and creamy. Stir in the milk, orange rind, and brandy.

Remove the waxed paper then pour the mixture into the pastry-lined pan. Bake at 450°F for 15 minute or until the edge of the crust is lightly browned. Reduce the heat to 300°F and bake 25 to 30 minutes longer.

While the pie is baking, make the meringue topping. Beat the egg whites until soft peaks form and then add the sugar. Beat until blended, about 2 to 3 minutes.

Lift the pie from the oven to the top of the stove and quickly spread with meringue. Be sure the meringue touches the crust all around and is smoothed or swirled over the top.

Return to the oven for 20 minutes longer to brown the meringue. (Keep an eye on it during browning phase!)

Remove the pie to a rack to cool 2 to 3 hours before cutting.

Sylvia Stoisor's Crêpes Suzette, contributed by Barbara Dan

SERVES 4

Sylvia Stoisor, who lived from 1900 to 1997, was my Rumanian mother-in-law. This is her favorite recipe for crêpes suzette, which she called clatite. It's simple to make and so delicious that family and friends will gobble up the crêpes faster than the cook can finish sautéing them. While every European country has its own version of crêpes suzette, this Rumanian recipe is so mouthwatering that I guarantee you plenty of compliments. While the crêpes are great for breakfast, they are even more fun as dessert.

1 cup flour, sifted
½ teaspoon salt
1 tablespoon sugar
4 eggs
1 cup milk, plus a tiny bit
    more
8–10 drops vanilla extract
Butter or margarine for
    cooking
Grape jelly, or any other
    kind of fruit jelly
Sour cream (optional)

Place the flour in a deep bowl. Add the salt and sugar in the middle of the flour and mix. Add the eggs, one at a time, mixing after each one until the batter is smooth and thoroughly blended.

Pour in the milk slowly, along with the drops of vanilla, stirring constantly and beating with a spoon. Add a tiny bit more milk and continue beating until the batter is thin and has no lumps.

Cover the batter and refrigerate 3 to 4 hours. (If you've used a blender to combine the above ingredients, you can begin making the crêpes right away.)

Use two large frying pans because the crêpes cook fast, and it's the easiest way to keep up with the demand. First melt a dab of butter in each pan. Then pour in just enough batter (about 2 tablespoons per pan) and swirl the pan, using your wrist to distribute the batter and make it as thin as possible.

Quickly tilt the pans to the right and left, taking care not to burn the crêpes. In seconds they will show signs of being cooked on one side. Flip them, and in no time the second side will be done.

Slide the cooked crêpe onto a large plate, and spread each pancake with a little jelly. Then roll up the entire crêpe and set it on a serving platter. Serve it with a dollop of sour cream—yummy, but optional.

Clay Reynolds's Aunt Minnie's Pound Cake

MAKES 1 BUNDT CAKE OR 2 LOAF CAKES

This recipe is fairly simple, but it's the best pound cake I've ever eaten, and I have testimony from everyone to whom it's been served that it qualifies for the same in their book as well. It was brought west from Kentucky by my great-great-great-aunt Minnie, who passed it down to my mother, who was brought up by this venerable lady, who reared seventeen children yet never had one of her own. Mother gave it to me. I added only the lemon zest to it, but that's really optional. It does give it a nice "zing" though.

Preheat the oven to 325°F. Grease and flour a large Bundt pan or two 1-pound loaf pans.

Combine the flour, salt, and baking soda and set aside.

In a large bowl, beat the butter and sugar until creamy, then add the eggs one at a time, beating well after each. Add alternately the lemon zest (if using it), flour mixture, vanilla, and sour cream, blending thoroughly after each addition.

Pour the batter into the greased and floured Bundt pan or two loaf pans. Bake for 90 minutes or until an inserted toothpick comes out clean.

Remove the cake from the oven and allow it to cool for 1 hour before turning out. Serve with fruit or ice cream or whipped cream. It's very rich.

3 cups flour
¼ teaspoon salt
¼ teaspoon baking soda
1 cup butter, softened
3 cups sugar
6 eggs
Zest of 1 lemon (optional)
2 teaspoons vanilla extract
1 cup sour cream

Anne Hillerman's Santa Fe Carrot Cake

MAKES 2 9-INCH CAKES

There are millions of carrot cake recipes, of course, just like there are millions of ways to write a great sentence. This one is based on the dessert served at a sweet little cafe I discovered as restaurant critic for *Journal Santa Fe*. The restaurant itself, now gone, made its home in an old adobe hacienda with a patio shaded by apricot trees in the summer. It sat on a one-way street about a block from the historic San Miguel Mission, the oldest church in the United States. In addition to their rich, moist cake, the restaurant served wonderful coffee and great pies. Just down the street from the State Capitol and less than a block from a building that hosted all kinds of state offices, the cafe made a great place to observe politics in action.

For the cake:
2 cups flour
1 cup sugar
1 teaspoon salt
1 teaspoon baking powder
1 teaspoon ground
   cinnamon
1 tablespoon vanilla extract
3 eggs
1 cup buttermilk
1 cup canola or vegetable
   oil
1 cup chopped pineapple
1 cup chopped mandarin
   oranges
2 cups shredded carrots
½ cup raisins
½ cup walnuts, chopped
Butter and flour for
   greasing the pans

Preheat the oven to 350°F. Lightly grease two 9-inch cake pans with butter and flour.

In a medium bowl, combine the dry ingredients. In another medium bowl, beat together the vanilla, eggs, buttermilk, and oil. Combine the two mixtures and beat lightly.

Add the fruits, carrot, raisins, and walnuts and stir to blend. Pour the batter into the pans and bake for 45 minutes or until set. (Test with a toothpick; it should come out dry.)

Combine the cream cheese, heavy cream, powdered sugar, and lemon or lime juice; stir until smooth. Frost the cake and sprinkle the top with walnuts.

About the altitude: This recipe works great at my Santa Fe home elevation of 7,000 feet. If you are baking at sea level, you will want to slightly decrease the flour and the liquid (the buttermilk), increase the baking powder, and bake the cake at 325°F.

For the frosting:

16 ounces cream cheese, room temperature

¼ cup heavy cream, room temperature

3 cups powdered sugar

1 teaspoon lemon or lime juice

2 cups walnuts, chopped

Tammy Hinton's Banana Pudding

SERVES 6–8

As I became an adult, I realized that the way my mother expressed her love was through desserts. Every Saturday morning after we cleaned house, Mama, my sister, and I would make a week's worth of baked goods for our family. Scratch recipes, of course. Usually, Dona and I served on the cookie brigade, but sometimes we could make something really special like banana pudding.

The real thrill of making banana pudding was that you not only got to lick the beaters but could also eat the broken vanilla wafers. I still do, and it makes me think of those Saturdays when I was a kid in Mama's kitchen.

1 (3.4-ounce) box instant vanilla pudding
1 (3.4-ounce) box instant banana pudding
3 cups milk
8 ounces cream cheese, softened
⅓ cup powdered sugar
8 ounces Cool Whip
3 bananas, sliced
Vanilla wafers

Mix the puddings with the milk in a large bowl. In a small bowl, blend the softened cream cheese and powdered sugar, and fold into the pudding. Next, fold in the Cool Whip. Add the bananas.

Layer the pudding mixture and vanilla wafers in a bowl, alternating a pudding layer with a wafer layer until the pudding is gone.

Tammy Hinton's Mama's Ginger Cookies

MAKES 2 DOZEN COOKIES

These cookies make the house smell so sweet and warm. My cousins still remark on how wonderful Aunt Louise's cookies were during the holidays. Mama has passed but her baking lives on.

Preheat the oven to 375°F.

Cream the 1 cup of sugar and shortening. Add the egg and molasses, then stir in the dry ingredients.

To form each cookie, roll about a tablespoon of dough into a ball, then roll the ball in some sugar. Place the balls on a cookie sheet and bake 8 to 10 minutes.

1 cup sugar, plus extra for rolling the dough balls
¾ cup shortening
1 egg
½ cup molasses
2 cups flour
2 teaspoons baking soda
¼ teaspoon salt
1 teaspoon ground cinnamon,
1 teaspoon ground ginger
1 teaspoon ground cloves

Quackgrass Sally's Mom's Perfect Piecrust

MAKES 2–4 CRUSTS, DEPENDING ON THE SIZE

Mom used to make yummy pies (my favorite being pumpkin for my birthday), but the best part of this crust recipe is when she would roll out a thin, flat piece and butter the top, sprinkle it with cinnamon and sugar, and bake it on a piece of foil alongside the pie for a few minutes. It was a special treat made with Mom's love . . . and almost better than pie!

4 cups all-purpose (not instant or self-rising) flour

2 teaspoons salt

2 tablespoons sugar

1¾ cups solid vegetable shortening (not butter, lard, or margarine)

1 large egg

1 tablespoon white or cider vinegar

½ cup water

In a large bowl, mix the flour, salt, and sugar with a sturdy fork. Add the shortening and continue to mix with the fork or a pastry cutter, until the mixture is crumbly.

In a small bowl, mix the egg, vinegar, and water until the egg is broken down. Combine the wet mixture with the flour mixture, and stir this until it is well mixed.

Knead the dough with your hands until it forms a smooth ball. Do not over-knead or the crust will become tough. The dough can be worked now with a floured rolling pin on a floured surface.

For easier rolling, divide the dough into 4 equal balls, flatten them, and wrap them with plastic wrap. Refrigerate the balls at least 30 minutes. You can also freeze the balls for later use. (Frozen crust takes about 3 hours to thaw.)

This crust works great for two-crusted pies or bake-and-fill crusts. It can be rolled out many times and still be flaky!

Stephen Bly's Pooch,
contributed by Janet Chester Bly

SERVES A 4-MAN TRAIL CREW

What? You expected more specific cowboy dessert recipe instructions? You must be kidding! These are the real deal, fresh off the trail. For the most part, bacon and salt pork dominated the menu. Any variety in food for a hungry cowboy could be mighty tasty. By the late 1880s, such foods as peaches and tomatoes appeared in air-tights, or cans. More ways for the camp cooks to create extras. Pooch sometimes subbed as a bready snack or dessert. Stephen Bly's southern grand-mother made a similar dish.

Mix together the tomatoes, sugar, and bread or biscuit cubes.

Cook this over the campfire until firm. Or pour it into a 9-inch square pan with a stick's worth of melted butter on the bottom and bake at 400°F about 30 minutes.

Serve this genuine cowboy treat warm.

Canned tomatoes
White or brown sugar, to taste
Bread or biscuits, in cubes
1 stick butter

Stephen Bly's Favorite Original Old-Fashioned Mincemeat Pie, contributed by Janet Chester Bly

MAKES 15 QUARTS TO KEEP ALL YEAR LONG IN THE ROOT CELLAR OR ANY PANTRY

When widow Leatha Jarnagin of the small village of Winchester, Idaho, learned that local Western author Stephen Bly's favorite pie was mincemeat, she baked from scratch for him every Christmas an old-fashioned pie like the one in this recipe. The rest of the Bly family preferred the sweet, less meaty-textured kind that spooned from a jar and that merited only a bite or two on rare occasions. To make Original Old-Fashioned Mincemeat Pie, you'll need to start weeks ahead.

4 boiled beef tongues or venison

4 pounds sugar

2 pounds raisins

2 pounds currants

½ pound candied citron peel, finely cut

6 pounds tart Granny Smith apples

1 tablespoon cinnamon, ground

1 tablespoon cloves, ground

2 whole nutmegs, grated

2½ pounds suet, finely chopped

½ pound candied orange peel, finely cut

½ pound candied lemon peel, finely cut

½ pound almonds, finely chopped

1 tablespoon salt

4 oranges, grated peel and juice

4 lemons, grated peel and juice

1 quart brandy (optional)

2 quarts whiskey (optional)

Chop the boiled beef tongues or deer meat very fine. Add the sugar, raisins, currants, and citron, and mix everything together well.

Finely chop the apples (do not mash), and add them to the meat mixture. Add all the spices, suet, candied peels, almonds, and salt. Mix thoroughly.

Grate the peels of the oranges and lemons and squeeze the oranges and lemons for their juice. Add the grated peels and fruit juices, plus the brandy and whiskey, to the rest of the ingredients and mix them together.

Place the mixture in a large crock. Cover the crock with a clean cloth and then cover it with a lid. Keep the crock in a cool place for 3 weeks, then add more salt and spices, if needed. Let the mixture stand for at least 4 weeks before using it for pies, cookies, etc.

Shanna Hatfield's Seven Layer Bar Cake

SERVES APPROXIMATELY 12

I am a Bundt cake junkie. There, I admitted it. I feel so much better now. An experiment with a can of sweetened condensed milk and a vanilla Bundt cake provided the inspiration for this delicious, decadent, divine cake. If you have even a passing fondness for seven layer bars, run into your kitchen and make this cake immediately.

Yes, seven layer bars—those incredibly yummy bar cookies with coconut, pecans, chocolate and butterscotch chips, and sweetened condensed milk over a graham cracker crust. Instead of a graham cracker crust, I substituted a rich, moist, chocolaty cake. If you take the plunge, your taste buds will dance in elation. In writing and baking, the best ingredient is love . . . unless you have chocolate.

Preheat the oven to 350°F.

Combine the first six ingredients in a large mixing bowl. Mix on medium speed until the ingredients are well blended. The batter will be really thick.

Thoroughly spray a Bundt pan with nonstick cooking spray. When you think you've coated every crevice, give it one more spray!

Pour the sweetened condensed milk into the bottom of the Bundt pan. Sprinkle on the pecans, followed by the butterscotch chips, chocolate chips, and coconut. Last, spoon in the cake batter.

Bake 1 hour or until a toothpick inserted near the center comes out clean. Do not overbake!

Let the cake cool completely before turning it over onto a serving platter or cake plate. Prepare to dazzle your guests and have to beat off a few of them with a stick when they get a taste of this cake!

1 (18-ounce) box chocolate cake mix
1 (3.4-ounce) box instant chocolate pudding
1 cup sour cream
½ cup water
½ cup oil, canola, peanut, or coconut will work
3 large eggs
1 (14-ounce) can sweetened condensed milk
½ cup chopped pecans
1 cup butterscotch chips
1 cup chocolate chips
1 cup coconut, shredded

G. R. (Honest Doc) Williamson's Mexican Bread Pudding

SERVES 6–8

This is my signature dish. I developed it to enter a contest for romantic dishes served in bed-and-breakfasts. Unilever, the manufacturer of I Can't Believe It's Not Butter!, planned to publish a book, tentatively titled *Fabio's I Can't Believe It's Not Butter! Romantic Recipes*. My recipe won second place in the contest, and I figured it was worth a bundle in free publicity. Wrong!

Before the book was finalized, Fabio was hit in the head by a goose while filming on a roller coaster at Busch Gardens, Virginia. Lawsuits followed and the book was scrapped. So much for the publicity, but it's still a killer dish.

½ cup dried apricots, chopped
1 stick butter, melted
1 loaf French bread, cut into 2-inch cubes
½ cup sugar
4 large eggs
2 cups milk
2 teaspoons vanilla extract
¼ teaspoon salt
1 teaspoon cinnamon

Preheat the oven to 375°F.

Place the apricots in a glass bowl and pour just enough water over them to cover them. Microwave for 2 minutes and set aside.

Melt the butter. Pour half of the butter into a glass 8 x 12 x 2-inch baking pan. Spread the bread cubes over the bottom of the pan. Place the pan in the oven for 15 minutes.

In a large bowl, cream the sugar into the rest of the butter. Beat in the eggs and then the milk, vanilla, and salt. Set this aside.

Remove the bread cubes from the oven. Drain the apricots, sprinkle them with cinnamon, and pour them over the bread cubes. Then evenly pour the sugar/egg/milk mixture over the bread mixture in the pan.

Place the glass pan inside a bigger metal baking pan that has ½ inch of water on the bottom. Loosely cover all of it with aluminum foil and bake for 20 minutes.

Remove the foil and bake an additional 15 to 20 minutes, or until a toothpick inserted into the center comes out dry. Remove the pan from the oven and let the pudding cool for 20 minutes. Spoon Cajeta Sauce (next page) over the bread pudding.

Cajeta Sauce

In a large glass bowl, mix the brown sugar with the apricot nectar. Microwave this mixture on high for 3 minutes.

Stir in the chopped pecans and coconut flakes. Microwave this for an additional 3 minutes.

Remove the mixture from the microwave and stir in the apricot brandy.

1 cup packed brown sugar
¼ cup apricot nectar
½ cup pecans, chopped
½ cup coconut flakes
3 tablespoons apricot
   brandy

Shoni Maulding's Chocolate Chip Pie

SERVES 6

This was originally my Aunt Linda's Hershey bar pie, when the candy was 5 cents each. Ron, my husband, and I live in the country, so when I didn't have Hershey bars, I substituted chocolate chips. Then I substituted real whipped cream for the frozen, prepared stuff because real whipped cream is better. When I didn't have graham crackers for the crust, I substituted animal crackers, and I use them exclusively now. Mom had brought a huge bag to me, saying that she knew I liked them. I was wondering what she was talking about, thinking dementia on her part. Later, she said that as a kid, I liked animal crackers. Now Mom really does have dementia, so I'm glad I substituted her original package for piecrust, and I continue to do so. It reminds me of her. And the chocolate part reminds me of my Aunt Linda.

1 cup chocolate chips
20 large marshmallows
¼ cup milk
½ pint cream, whipped
1 Animal Cracker Piecrust (You may also use a ready-made graham cracker piecrust.)

Put the chocolate chips, marshmallows, and milk in a saucepan over medium-high heat. Stir constantly so the mixture doesn't burn and the ingredients are mixed thoroughly.

Cool the mixture, making sure that it does not become too cool and stiff to mix in the whipped cream.

Whip the cream and fold it into the melted mixture. Pour it into the piecrust. Chill the pie for several hours before serving.

Animal Cracker Piecrust

¼ cup sugar
½ cup butter, melted
1½ cups animal crackers, crushed

Add the sugar and butter to the animal crackers and stir until the crumbs are moist.

Put the mixture in a pie pan and press it into the pan with your fingers. Bake the crust 10 minutes at 350°F. Let it cool before adding the pie filling.

Susan D. Matley's The Family Fudge

MAKES ABOUT 1 POUND

This recipe might appear in several cookbooks, but I learned it from my dad, who learned it from his dad. All of us were born in Washington State. That might qualify this as a Western recipe, but if it needs additional credentials, I was shown how to make The Family Fudge one night when we were watching a new episode of the 1960s series *Batman*. If this reference makes you scratch your head, remember: The title role was played by Adam WEST.

In a heavy 3-quart saucepan, combine the sugar, milk, and unsweetened chocolate. Bring the mixture to a rolling boil over medium-high heat. Reduce the heat and continue boiling (stirring rarely, if ever) until the mixture reaches soft-ball stage. To test this, use a metal spoon to drip a few drops of the mixture into a glass of cold water; when ready, the mixture will form a soft ball as it settles in the bottom of the glass.

Remove the mixture from the heat. Add the vanilla and butter (the vanilla will make an entertaining, fizzling noise). With a handheld electric mixer, beat the mixture on low speed until it thickens and starts to lose its sheen. Stir in the walnuts, if desired. Pour the fudge onto a greased plate. Let it cool at room temperature until it is firm enough to cut.

2 cups white granulated sugar
⅞ cup milk (I use 2%.)
3 ounces unsweetened chocolate
1 teaspoon vanilla extract
2 tablespoons butter
1 cup chopped walnuts (optional)

Cowboy Mike's Pinto Bean Cake

SERVES 12–16

As the sun began to drop on the trail west of Lubbock, Texas, on the Llano Estacado, I found a good spot to set camp. As I unsaddled my horse, Jaguar, the pack mule that carried all of my cooking gear began to bray. Some cowboys ride light with just a few hard biscuits and raw bacon in their saddlebags. I always liked to eat as well on the trail as I would at the ranch. I also love to cook. So, I unpacked my gear and my cooking utensils and started a campfire . . . It was at this time that a grizzled old cowboy who looked down on his luck rode into my camp. I was just preparing some grub when we crossed paths. As a friendly cowboy gesture, I asked if he cared to join me. That old cowpoke was half bent over and looked as if he hadn't eaten in a month of Sundays. He wore a beaver lid that defied age. I wasn't sure if it dated back to the 1920s or the 1820s. He said his name was Slim . . . Without a single moment of hesitation, Slim reached over and scooped the rabbit stew and a biscuit onto a tin pie plate. The food was as hot as West Texas with a visible ray of heat rising from it. However, it wasn't just the fire that made the stew hot. Slim did not know that my secret ingredient was chili peppers that I added to most everything I cooked . . . His first words after eating this fill was, "Cowboy Mike, where did you learn to cook like that? I've never had rabbit pie that tasted so good."

I said that back in Georgia where I hailed from and was renowned for my cooking. Well, he said, "I bet I got a dish that you've never heard of or fixed before." I waited to hear what Slim had to say and wondered what this old stoved-up cowboy knew about cooking. It was then that he told me that in days past he was the cookie (chuckwagon cook) for a big outfit near Pampa, Texas. He waxed eloquent about Son-of-a-Gun Stew, Mountain Oysters, Crisped Marrow-Gut, and Blanket Steaks.

After about twenty minutes of hearing the food he cooked and the way cowboys ate, I was convinced that Slim might have a recipe that was unknown to me. It was at this point that Slim told me about Pinto Bean Cake. I laughed when I heard the name, but as he began to share with me how it was put together, it made sense. Well we laughed and talked most of the night, and as Slim rode off the next morning, I told him that I would share his recipe with my friends and neighbors, and this is what I have done over the years.

Preheat the oven to 350°F.

In a large bowl, cream the sugar and butter until light and fluffy. Add the eggs and mix well.

Sift all the dry ingredients together in a small bowl. Next, add the beans and dry ingredients to the creamed sugar mixture. Mix well and then stir in the pecans.

Pour into a lightly greased and floured 13 x 9 x 2-inch pan (or a Cowboy Mike 10-inch cast-iron skillet). Bake for 50 to 60 minutes or until the cake tests done with a toothpick. Cool before frosting with Butter Icing (below).

2 cups sugar
½ cup soft butter
2 eggs
1¼ cups all-purpose flour
½ teaspoon allspice
1 tablespoon cocoa powder
½ teaspoon baking powder
1 teaspoon cinnamon
1 teaspoon baking soda
2 cups cooked pinto beans, mashed and whipped until fluffy
½ cup chopped pecans

Butter Icing

Cream the butter and sugar in a large bowl and then stir in the vanilla and milk. Beat until smooth and of spreading consistency.

Spread the icing evenly on the cooled cake. Sprinkle the top with coarsely chopped nuts, if desired.

⅓ cup soft butter
3 cups powdered sugar
1¼ teaspoons vanilla extract
1–2 tablespoons milk
Nuts, chopped for topping (optional)

Vicky Rose's Texas Sheet Cake, with Two Icing Variations

SERVES 20

Fifty years ago, there was a woman where I lived who made cakes for a living. Mrs. Woods kept her caramel icing recipe a closely guarded secret, and only a few women in town knew how to make it. My ex-mother-in-law somehow obtained a copy and shared it with me. It doesn't make a pretty cake, but it makes a delicious one. A friend once told me her grandmother advised that "you have to hold your mouth just right when you make it." The cake below is my recipe, and it's easy. It's the caramel icing that gives so much trouble.

2 cups all-purpose flour
2 cups sugar
½ teaspoon salt
1 cup water
1 stick (½ cup) butter
½ cup shortening
3 tablespoons cocoa
½ cup buttermilk★
½ teaspoon baking soda
2 eggs
1 teaspoon vanilla extract

★ Use whole buttermilk, not low-fat. Do not substitute the buttermilk with a mixture of whole milk and a tablespoon of lemon juice, as some recipes allow.

Preheat the oven to 375°F.

Mix together the flour, sugar, and salt and set it aside. Bring to a boil the water, butter, shortening, and cocoa. Then pour the boiling liquid over the dry ingredients.

Add the buttermilk, baking soda, eggs, and vanilla and mix well. Pour the batter into a 9 x 13-inch greased sheet cake pan. (I like using baking spray instead of greasing or buttering.)

Bake the cake for 25 to 30 minutes, or until an inserted toothpick comes out with just a few crumbs on it. This cake will taste better the second day.

Chocolate Icing

Bring the milk, cocoa, and butter to a boil and remove it from the heat. Add the powdered sugar and vanilla and beat well. If you feel it is too thin, add more powdered sugar. Add the pecans.

Spread the icing over the warm cake while it is still in the pan.

6 tablespoons milk
3 tablespoons cocoa
⅔ stick (⅓ cup) butter
4 cups powdered (confectioners') sugar
1 teaspoon vanilla extract
½ cup pecans, chopped

Caramel Icing

In a heavy 3-quart saucepan, combine the 2 cups of sugar, milk, butter, and corn syrup. Place the pan over medium-low heat and mix well.

While this cooks, take a small heavy skillet or saucepan and in it melt 3 heaping tablespoons of sugar over low heat. As the sugar begins to melt, stir constantly to keep it from burning.

Once the melted sugar has turned a dark golden brown (not too brown, because you don't want it to burn!), pour it into the boiling liquid in the other pot. It must be boiling so the ingredients in both pots mix together well. If you want to get technical, cook it to just below soft-ball stage, about 230°F.

Remove the pot from the heat and add the vanilla. Let the icing cool a little bit and then start beating. Once the icing has thickened, spread it over the cooled cake.

2 cups sugar, plus 3 heaping tablespoons
½ cup milk
1 stick (½ cup) butter
2 tablespoons white corn syrup
1 teaspoon vanilla extract

Sherry Monahan's Apple Pie

SERVES 6–8

Who doesn't love pie? Apple pie is just plain yummy! Heck, any kind of pie is in my mind. One day I'm gonna write a book about pie in the West. My niece Jamie and I call ourselves "pie-rates" because we love pie so much. We hold a spoon sideways over one eye for a patch before we eat and then giggle. Don't ask me my favorite flavor because I'll tell you pecan, cherry, coconut cream, lemon, key lime, peach, pumpkin, German chocolate, and well, you get the point.

4–6 tart apples, peeled, cored, and sliced
¼–½ cup sugar
½ teaspoon cinnamon
¼ teaspoon salt
¼ cup flour
Butter, cut into ¼-inch squares
2 piecrusts (see recipe on next page

Preheat the oven to 350°F.

Line a 9- or 10-inch pie pan with one crust.

Combine the apples, sugar, cinnamon, salt, and flour in a bowl. Stir to coat the apples evenly.

Pour the apples into the piecrust. Place a few pieces of butter around the pie and cover with the second crust.

Bake for about 40 minutes, or until the apples are tender. Serve with ice cream or whipped cream.

Sherry Monahan's Aunt Anna's Piecrust

MAKES 2 9-INCH CRUSTS

My family has guarded this recipe closely for decades. My father gave it to me, and he learned it from his sister Anna. I shared this in my very first book, *Taste of Tombstone*, with her permission, because it's the best darned piecrust recipe ever. This recipe is so good that my husband's aunt Alice always asked me to make her just the crust, with no filling to get in the way of its great taste.

Combine the flour, baking powder, and salt in a large mixing bowl, stirring with a wire whisk. Cut in the shortening with a pastry cutter and blend until the dough resembles crumbs.

Break the egg into a liquid measuring cup and beat lightly. Add the vinegar and enough water to measure ⅓ cup on the measuring cup. Stir well. Add this to the flour and shortening mixture. Stir only enough to moisten and combine. Overmixing will result in a tough crust. If the dough seems too wet, add a little more flour.

Divide the dough in half and roll out on a floured surface. Makes two 9-inch piecrusts.

Note: To make a sweeter crust, add 1 tablespoon of sugar and ½ teaspoon of cinnamon to the flour mix. You can also cut this recipe in half to make a single crust.

2½ cups flour
1½ teaspoons baking powder
½ teaspoon salt
¾ cup shortening or lard
1 egg
½ teaspoon vinegar
Cold water

Meg Mims's Famous Pistachio Cake

SERVES 8–12

I love cake! Frosted, glazed, powdered, for any occasion. This recipe is adapted from my mother-in-law, who often made it for church suppers and potlucks. I wanted to replace the vegetable oil, since the original recipe called for ½ cup, so I experimented until I could substitute the right amount of applesauce. It works nicely. The pistachio flavor and dense, rich, buttery cake are a perfect match. This cake is always a hit, and if there are any leftovers, I will nibble away while writing . . . if my husband doesn't get them first.

4 eggs
⅓ cup oil
4 ounces applesauce
1 cup sour cream
1 (15–16.5) ounce box
   Butter Golden Cake Mix
1 (3.4-ounce) box instant
   pistachio pudding
½ cup powdered sugar
Pistachio nuts, chopped

Preheat the oven to 350°F. Spray a Bundt pan with baking spray or grease with shortening.

Beat all the ingredients, except the powdered sugar and chopped pistachios, together on low, then beat for 2 minutes on medium. Pour the batter into the pan.

Bake for 50 to 55 minutes. Test for doneness with a toothpick. Cool the cake in the pan, and then turn it out onto a plate.

Sprinkle the cake with powdered sugar or spread a glaze over the top. (The glaze is made by mixing ½ cup powdered sugar with 1 teaspoon or more of water.) After sprinkling the powdered sugar or spreading the glaze, sprinkle chopped pistachios on top.

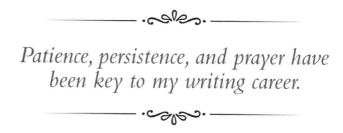

Patience, persistence, and prayer have been key to my writing career.

Meg Mims's Famous Nine-Lemon Icebox Pie

SERVES 8–10

The key to a man's love is through his stomach, or so I was always told. I decided to try my future mother-in-law's Lemon Icebox Pie recipe, who always made it "extra lemony." For a 9-inch pie, I juiced nine lemons and had to add a ton of cornstarch to thicken it. Oh my! After taking a bite, my future husband and two friends kissed their tonsils and laughed so hard, their throats nearly closed up! (And no wonder I write murder mysteries.) After that, I cut down the lemon juice to two-thirds of a cup. Ahem.

For the homemade crust:
Mix all the ingredients together. Press the mixture into a pie dish. Bake the crust 5 minutes at 350°F, and then let it cool. You can also use a ready-made graham cracker crust.

For the filling:
Beat the egg yolks 5 to 8 minutes, until they are light and thick. Stir in the remaining ingredients. Pour the mixture into the crust.

For the meringue:
Beat the egg whites and cream of tartar on high until foamy. Then gradually add the sugar, while beating to firm peaks. Spread the meringue over the filling and brown the pie in a 375°F oven for 10 to 12 minutes.

Chill the pie in the refrigerator for several hours or overnight before serving.

For the homemade crust:
¼ cup sugar
¼ cup butter, melted
20 graham crackers, crushed

For the filling:
4 eggs yolks
⅛ teaspoon salt
1 (14-ounce) can sweetened
    condensed milk
1 teaspoon lemon rind
⅔ cup lemon juice

For the meringue:
4 egg whites
½ teaspoon cream of tartar
½ cup sugar

Joyce Lohse's Lizzie's Lemon Cookies

MAKES 30–40 COOKIES

A similar cookie recipe was among notes written by Baby Doe Tabor, I discovered during my research for Lizzie's biography. Her real name was Elizabeth McCourt Doe Tabor, and she was known as Lizzie to family and friends. A similar recipe also appeared in her copy of the 1887 *White House Cook Book*. I adapted and adjusted the recipe to modern style, with measured ingredients.

¼ teaspoon baking soda
1¼ teaspoons milk
2½ cups flour, sifted
  (Save ½ cup to dust the
  rolling pin and board.)
½ cup butter, softened
1 cup sugar
Juice from 1 small lemon,
  or 2 tablespoons
Peel from the lemon, finely
  grated
2 eggs, beaten

Preheat the oven to 350°F.

Mix the baking soda and milk, and then combine with the rest of the ingredients, after setting aside ½ cup flour.

Roll the dough out flat and thin with a flour-dusted rolling pin. Use an inverted shot glass or a small cookie cutter to cut the dough into rounds.

Bake the cookies plain, or decorate each one with a raisin, nut, or a sprinkle of brown sugar and cinnamon. Bake the cookies on a flat cookie sheet lined with parchment paper for 10 minutes. Let the cookies cool before placing them in a storage container.

Joyce Lohse's Molly Brown Molasses Drop Cakes

MAKES 25–35 COOKIES

Cookies supposedly evolved from cake-like dough dropped on top of the woodstove to determine its baking temperature. A version of this recipe appeared in the *1896 Fannie Farmer Cookbook*. This treat could have been served in Margaret Brown's Denver mansion, which was often full of children and lively activity. I sometimes serve these cookies at book events for *Unsinkable: The Molly Brown Story*.

Preheat the oven to 350°F.

Mix the molasses, butter, and sugar in a large bowl. Add the baking soda and beat thoroughly. Then add the water and egg.

Into a separate bowl, sift together the flour, ginger, cinnamon, and salt. Add the flour mixture to the batter.

Drop the batter by the spoonful on a prepared baking sheet (I line mine with parchment paper).

Bake 12 to 15 minutes, until golden brown. Remove the cookies from the oven, and let them cool.

1 cup molasses
½ cup butter, melted
1 cup sugar
2 teaspoons baking soda
1 cup hot water
1 egg, well beaten
4 cups flour
2 teaspoons ginger, ground
1 teaspoon cinnamon, ground
½ teaspoon salt

Michael Zimmer's Kentucky Butter Cake

SERVES 10–12

We found this one through some rendezvous friends. Rich and decadent. If the mountain men had had this, they would have been trading plews for slices of cake.

3 cups flour (If using self-rising flour, omit the baking powder, salt, and baking soda.)
1 teaspoon baking powder
1 teaspoon salt
½ teaspoon baking soda
1 cup butter, room temperature
2 cups sugar
4 eggs
1 cup buttermilk
2 teaspoons vanilla extract

Preheat the oven to 325°F.

Sift together the flour, baking powder, salt, and baking soda.

In a separate bowl, cream together the butter, sugar (added gradually), and eggs.

Combine the buttermilk and vanilla in a bowl or glass measuring cup for easy pouring.

Add the buttermilk mixture, alternating with the dry ingredients, to the cream mixture, beginning and ending with the dry. Blend well after each addition.

Pour the batter into a 10-inch tube pan or Bundt pan, greased on the bottom. Bake for 60 to 65 minutes, or until the top springs back when touched in the center.

Run a spatula around the edges and stem of the pan. Pierce the cake (an ice pick works here, if you don't have a Bowie knife) and pour warm sauce (see below) over the cake. Let the cake cool before removing it from the pan.

Sauce

1 cup sugar
¼ cup water
½ cup butter
1 tablespoon vanilla extract

Combine the sugar, water, and butter. Heat the mixture just until melted. Add the vanilla.

Michael Zimmer's Homemade Ice Cream

SERVES 6–8

Everyone has a favorite ice cream recipe. This is ours, passed down through several generations of my wife Vanessa's family. The more eggs, the richer the ice cream.

Fill a 2- or 3-quart saucepan with the eggs, sugar, and half-and-half. Fill the rest of the pan with milk and heat. Add the Junket tablets and vanilla extract.

Pour the mixture into a freezer container and fill the container to the fill line with more milk. Stir the mixture and cool it before freezing.

3–12 eggs
2 cups sugar
1 quart half-and-half
Milk
4 Junket (rennet) tablets
1 tablespoon vanilla extract

Chapter Six

Roundup
(Sauces, Salsas, and
Other Extras)

Western Writers of America publishes a bi-monthly magazine called Roundup™, so we thought it would be fun to name this chapter after the magazine. The magazine includes something for everyone in each issue—a letter from our president, book reviews, articles on technology, movies, history, research, upcoming events, and more. We also have unique features in each publication. See? There is a little of everything. Like the magazine, this chapter includes a little bit of everything, so we thought we'd give a shout-out to Roundup™ by using its name.

In writing, it's often the little things that are memorable—weird details about a historical event or odd personality quirks of a character. The same is true with food. The extras often provide the standout moments of your day. So sip a hot toddy, dip some chips in a spicy salsa, or munch on sweetened carrot sticks. And don't forget the oat cakes for your horse!

JoJo Thoreau's Butterale Tea

SERVES 1–2

I grew up in a cold northeastern region, and this drink has always been a family favorite. After long hours of playing in the snow, there is nothing any better than coming inside to warm up with a delicious-smelling cup of hot butterale tea. This recipe also creates warm holiday memories when enjoyed on Christmas Eve while reading Clement Clarke Moore's *'Twas the Night before Christmas*. Not able to get your little buckaroos to drink liquids when they have a cold? Try this recipe to offer them the yummiest natural remedy for a cold—they'll enjoy its apple pie flavor.

2 cups ginger ale
1 teaspoon butter
1 tablespoon brown sugar
¼ teaspoon cinnamon
1 teaspoon honey, or 2
  teaspoons to soothe a
  sore throat

Pour the ginger ale into a 2-cup microwave-safe measuring cup. Microwave on high until the soda is hot but not boiling, 1 to 2 minutes. Gently stir in the butter to melt, then stir in the brown sugar, cinnamon, and honey. Be sure to stir gently to avoid the soda fizzing up. Pour the drink into mugs, and serve. You can adjust the butter, sugar, and honey amounts to suit your own taste.

Dennis McCown's Cowboy Coffee

SERVES ABOUT 2

I can't drink caffeinated coffee anymore. Something about my heart, they say . . . or maybe it was my cholesterol. But think about it: In the Old West, the water was sometimes unsafe. The only liquid a cowboy might intake was this stuff: hard as horseshoes, rough as cactus going down your throat, cup after cup, all day. No wonder these cowboys sometimes did shots of whiskey for recreation!

Put the coffee and water in a large enameled coffeepot or in a large saucepan. Place the pot near the coals in a campfire or on the stove. Let the coffee and water simmer a minimum of 30 minutes. Add more water as the cowboys come in. Using a strainer (or coffee filter), pour the coffee into cups. Add 4 teaspoons of brown sugar to each cup.

Optional: In cold weather or other adverse conditions, add 2 shots of Old Overholt rye whiskey—a cowboy favorite.

1 handful of Arbuckle's ground coffee
1 gallon of well water or non-muddy river flow
4–12 teaspoons of brown sugar

Shoni Maulding's Frappe, the Homemade Cheap One

SERVES 1, OR 2 IF YOU'RE APT TO SHARE

I don't drink coffee, which is horrific in my husband's opinion, and probably not the Western way to do things. Coffee gives me the shakes. But my stepdaughter, Becky, got me hooked on a name-brand frappucino. I'm too cheap to spend the $$$, though, unless I'm with Becky. I found this sorta recipe in a magazine, but I had to change it around. I dropped the sugar (why bother?) and added way more chocolate syrup than the recipe called for. Way more . . . If it's gonna be chocolate, then it has to scream CHOCOLATE! I've been known to count up to 40, or as low as 26, as I'm pouring in the syrup. That part is up to you. This drink is a great pick-me-up in the afternoon. Now I like it better than any store-bought drink, and I don't have to drive to town to buy it.

⅓ cup brewed coffee
⅓ cup milk
Chocolate syrup
8 ice cubes

Put the coffee and milk in a blender that can crush ice. Add the chocolate syrup. Don't bother measuring, but just count to 30 as the chocolate swirls from the container into the blender. Add the ice cubes. Blend until the ice is crushed, then pour the drink into a glass and eat it with a spoon. Toward the bottom of the glass, the drink will be more like a mixture of cold coffee, milk, and chocolate, but it is still refreshing.

With technical writing: Write from the perspective of someone who can't learn from a how-to book. It helps if you're one of those people.

Susan Union's Five Drinks Recipes

ALL RECIPES ARE SINGLE SERVINGS, BUT DON'T DRINK ALONE!

These drink recipes are from my mystery novel *Rode to Death*, set in the gritty yet glamorous world of quarter horse breeding. All are featured in the book's neighborhood bar, the Surf & Stirrup, and were drunk by real characters! This fictional watering hole is on the beach in north San Diego County and caters to the surf crowd, wealthy Western horse-owners, barn workers, racetrack patrons, and everyone in between.

Rattlesnake Cider is the perfect mix of sugar and spice. This mug of everything nice will warm you up after an evening of grunion hunting on the beach or a chilly desert night spent stargazing. Cowboy Cool-Aid allows you to chill out after a run on the beach or a hot day in the saddle. Nothing beats an ice-cold beer—especially one with a "kick" to it.

Saddle up for a wild time with a Mustang Mai-Tai. This tasty combination of sweet and sour brings to mind the islands, with a Western twist. My Tequila Sunset will prove that sunsets are better in the West. Take off your boots and hit the porch. Feeling stubborn? Need a little pick-me-up? Try my Mule Kick!

Susan Union's Rattlesnake Cider

MAKES 1 DRINK

Serve in a mug and top with whipped cream.

1 cup hot apple cider
1 shot Fireball whiskey
Dash of Tabasco

Susan Union's Tequila Sunset

MAKES 1 DRINK

Pour the tequila into a glass with ice. Fill it with orange or pineapple juice and stir well. Add the brandy. Top with the cherry.

1 shot tequila
Orange or pineapple juice
½ shot blackberry brandy
1 cherry, for garnish

Susan Union's Cowboy Cool-Aid

MAKES 1 DRINK

1 cup Pacifico or Corona
(It doesn't have to be
Mexican—any light-style
brew will do.)
½ cup lemonade
Dash of cayenne pepper

Pour this over ice in a pint glass with a salted rim.

Susan Union's Mustang Mai-Tai

MAKES 1 DRINK

1 lime, juiced
1 shot Gran Marnier
2 shots rum
½ shot Jagermeister
1 lime wedge, for garnish

Shake the ingredients with crushed ice. Pour the drink into a highball glass. Garnish with a lime wedge.

Susan Union's Mule Kick

MAKES 1 DRINK

2 shots espresso or black
coffee
1 shot Bailey's Irish Cream
1 shot vodka
1 mint leaf, for garnish

Pour the coffee into a mug. Add the Bailey's and vodka. Stir lightly and top with a mint leaf.

Quackgrass Sally's Dad's Tom & Jerry Hot Toddy Mix

MAKES OVER A QUART OF MIX, WHICH IS "DOZENS" OF YUMMY TODDIES!

My dad would make these, using his special brandy, when folks came over to our house in the winter months. Even we kids got our "toddy" (without the added spirits, of course) and we felt very grown-up! This makes a yummy, warm-your-tummy drink. Add a jigger or so of your favorite rum or brandy and . . . yahoooo, a great hot toddy for cold winter evenings around the fire.

Combine all the ingredients in a blender or large mixing bowl. Blend or stir until everything is well mixed and smooth. Pour the mixture into a tight-lidded container and freeze it until firm.

Fill a large coffee cup ¾ full with boiling water. Add 2 tablespoons of the hot toddy mix to the cup and stir.

1 cup melted butter
1 cup brown sugar
1 cup powdered sugar
1 teaspoon vanilla extract
1 teaspoon cinnamon
1 quart vanilla ice cream, slightly soft

Hank Corless's Silver City Salsa

MAKES ABOUT A HALF-GALLON, OR ENOUGH FOR ALL THE HANDS

I spent years perfecting this recipe from an original salsa recipe I picked up a few years ago in Mazatlán, Mexico. You can make it hotter or milder by altering the amount of jalapeños, cumin, and cayenne pepper, and you can adjust all the ingredients in this recipe to your preference. What I like about it is that it's authentic Mexican and not all watery or sloppy, so it doesn't easily drip down your keyboard. It allows me to have a pause for thought at the writing desk instead of stopping to fix lunch. Oftentimes I forego the chips and just eat it with a spoon.

7–8 Roma tomatoes, diced
1 medium yellow onion, diced
6 jalapeño peppers, diced
3 garlic cloves, finely chopped or minced
1 bunch cilantro, chopped
1 teaspoon cumin
½ teaspoon cayenne pepper
1 tablespoon ground pepper
1 teaspoon salt
½ cup lime juice

Combine the diced tomatoes, onion, and jalapeño peppers in a large bowl. Throw in the chopped garlic, along with the cilantro. Add the cumin, cayenne pepper, ground pepper, salt, and lime juice. Stir it all up with a big spoon, then place it in a refrigerator to chill for at least 1 hour before serving. Overnight chilling would be even better.

Sprinkling this with a little fine trail dust is authentic but optional, because we're not talkin' New York City here. Don't forget to have a big bowl of tortilla chips on the side or your favorite spoon!

Micki Fuhrman's Sweetfire Sauce

MAKES ½ CUP

This is a versatile hot and sweet sauce that can be used as a topping or marinade for meats. It is similar to a Jezebel sauce but does not contain mustard or horseradish. I serve it alongside spicy meat pies. I actually use a little more hot sauce than the recipe calls for, but then I'm originally from Louisiana!

Place all the ingredients in a microwave-safe mixing bowl. Microwave on high for 1 minute. Remove and blend with a whisk until the mixture is smooth. If necessary, microwave for an additional 30 seconds and blend again. It can also be heated on the stove in a saucepan over low heat for 5 to 10 minutes.

This sauce is excellent with meats (fried or grilled). The hot sauce amount may be adjusted to suit your palate.

4 ounces apple jelly

1 tablespoon Worcestershire sauce

1 teaspoon Louisiana Hot Sauce

Maybe it's my songwriting background, but I pay a lot of attention to first lines that put readers right in the middle of the story, and last lines that leave them with a smile or an ache (or both). Also, the story needs rhythm . . . crescendos and ebbs in action and tension level. "Picture" words are important to me. I labor over just the right verb or noun. (Yes, I'm a slow writer.)

Sherry Monahan's Pico de Gallo

SERVES 6–8

I love to cook and write! My passions of food, history, and writing (OK, wine, too!) have led me to create my nonfiction books about food, wine, and daily life in the American West. What better way to share history with people than through food and drink? Tasting history is so much better than just reading about it. While this recipe is not historic, it reminds me of the West whenever I make it. OK, it's historic in the fact that I don't measure and had to stop and think about it to share this recipe. Now, make a margarita or pour your favorite glass of red wine (mine is Zin or Petite Sirah) and enjoy.

6–8 Roma tomatoes, chopped
1 (14.5-ounce) can petite tomatoes
1 onion, chopped fine
1–4 jalapeño peppers, to taste
1–2 teaspoons salt
½ cup fresh chopped cilantro
½–1 lime, juiced
Corn tortilla chips

Combine all the ingredients, except for the chips, in a bowl and taste for heat and seasoning. The more lime juice you add, the more intense the pepper heat will become. It's always better to add salt and peppers in small increments. As my husband says, "You can always add more, but once it's in, you can't take it out!"

Serve with corn tortilla chips.

Find something you're passionate about, and the story flows.

Join a local or national writers' organization, like Western Writers of America, to network.

Start building a résumé by writing for free—it gets your name out there.

For nonfiction, become an expert in the field you write about.

Denzel Holmes's Unsweet Basting and Barbecue Sauce

SERVES 10 OR MORE

I have not measured my ingredients in years, knowing them by heart. You too can vary your amounts, but this is a good starting point. I despise sweet barbeque sauce, so I never add sugar or anything like it. Ketchup has some sugar, but you won't taste it in the sauce. I have no trouble drawing in the larger family when they know Denzel is cooking brisket.

Basting Sauce

Mix the above ingredients together, then boil gently for 1 hour. Apply the sauce to the meat before cooking, once during cooking, and once more after the meat is taken up. I prefer charcoal cooking, allowing about 1¼ hours per pound of meat (slow cooking). My specialty is beef brisket. This recipe will more than baste a single brisket that serves 10 people.

1 cup water
4 ounces Worcestershire sauce
4 ounces soy sauce
½ cup fresh parsley leaves
1 stick butter
1 ounce wine
2 cloves garlic, chopped or 2 teaspoons garlic powder

Barbecue Sauce

The basting sauce converts to a tasty barbeque sauce by taking what is left over from basting.

Stir in the ketchup with a whisk to break up the clumps. Boil the sauce for a few minutes to blend the ingredients. More of the original ingredients can be added in smaller quantities to build back to the volume you desire.

1 cup ketchup
2 teaspoons vinegar

Denzel Holmes's Simple Salsa

SERVES 20 OR MORE

After reading this recipe, you'll see I like hot salsa. I find that modern farm-grown jalapeño peppers are often as mild as bell peppers; therefore I add habaneros. The citric acid was a recent discovery, and it adds a bit of tanginess. As presented, this salsa is great on breakfast eggs in any form and will not give you breath that will drop a bull buffalo at twenty paces. Of course, you can build on the recipe with onions, garlic, oregano, etc. Look out, buffalo!

12 fresh jalapeño peppers
1 (28-ounce) can petite diced tomatoes
1 (10-ounce) can Ro-Tel
2 heaping teaspoons onion salt
2 habanero peppers, boiled and deseeded (optional)
1 teaspoon citric acid (optional)

Gently boil the jalapeño peppers for 10 minutes over medium heat. Wearing a vinyl glove on the hand handling the peppers, split, deseed, and destem them. Blend them briefly in a food processor.

Thoroughly drain the diced tomatoes and the Ro-Tel tomatoes and add them to the processor. Toss in the onion salt. Add habaneros and citric acid if using. Blend the mixture for only a few seconds, in short bursts. You're done.

This recipe makes enough to fill two 16-ounce plastic screw-on-top plastic containers. Freeze one and keep the other in the fridge.

Write from the heart; feel it.

Avoid adverbs and adjectives.

Make your characters engaging, not just interesting.

Never use the same noun or verb twice in a paragraph.
Same rule applies to most other words.

Everyone needs at least two editors.

Anne Hillerman's Santa Fe Green Chile Sauce

SERVES ABOUT 4

Green chile sauce is our family's go-to comfort food. My husband, my son, my step-kids, their kids, all crave this sauce. The amount of heat, which we call picante, depends on the chile itself. Chile grown in hot, dry years is spicier. If we end up with some that's too warm for our palates, we temper it with a touch of sour cream. You can turn this sauce into a stew with the addition of stew meat instead of the ground meat, and by adding potatoes, celery, and carrots to taste and more liquid.

Feel free to improvise with this recipe to get the flavor and sauciness you prefer. I've added chicken or beef stock. The only rule is that the natural flavor of the green chile must come through. You can also make this without meat; sauté the other ingredients first in olive or vegetable oil in that case before adding the green chiles.

Using a small Dutch oven or deep cast-iron skillet, brown the meat and add the onion and garlic when the meat is nearly done.

Add all the other ingredients. If using canned chiles, include the liquid. If using frozen, there's no need to defrost.

Simmer slowly until the potato is soft, adding broth to reach your own desired consistency for the sauce. Adjust the seasoning.

This sauce is great for huevos rancheros, enchiladas, burritos, or in a bowl with a few pinto beans and a fresh tortilla on the side.

1 pound ground pork or beef

1 yellow onion, diced

1 head garlic, minced or finely diced

28 ounces frozen, fresh, or canned green chiles, chopped (Use fresh roasted if you can find them.)

1 potato, cubed

1 tablespoon ground oregano

2–3 cups broth of your choice, as needed

Salt and pepper, to taste

Quentin Hulse's Surefire Red Hot Canyon Creek Red Chile Sauce, contributed by Nancy Coggeshall

MAKES A BUNCH

This is typically prepared in large batches for freezing. Quantities are determined by the size of the bag of chiles. Quentin Hulse was a renowned rancher/hunter/outfitter and guide in Catron County, New Mexico. He started cooking for hands at the age of twelve. His signature dishes reflected the cowboy cuisine of New Mexico's ranching Southwest: fried potatoes, beans with salt pork, red chile, beef brisket, sourdough biscuits, posole with hominy and pork, and menudo with pigs' feet. He is the subject of *Gila County Legend: The Life and Times of Quentin Hulse* and the song "Light on the Mountain," written and recorded by Wyoming's Dave Munsick.

1 (16-ounce) sack dried red chile pods
Water to cover
Garlic cloves, peeled, to taste
½–1 teaspoon cumin
½–1 teaspoon coriander
½–1 teaspoon oregano
⅓–½ cup shortening (could be bacon grease, margarine, or olive oil)
Handful of cilantro (optional)
2 tablespoons flour

Split and remove the pod cap, veins, and seeds from the chile pods. Crumble the pods, place them in a pressure cooker, cover them with water, and cook for 8 to 10 minutes. Be careful not to touch your eyes if you don't wear gloves.

Remove the pods from the heat and blend in batches of the raw garlic, to taste. After mixing, place the blended pods in a large stew pot, adding the cumin, coriander, oregano, and shortening. (Quentin suggested a "good handful" of cilantro as well.)

Bring the mixture to a low boil and simmer until everything is incorporated, taking care not to simmer too long, about 30 minutes. An extended cooking time lessens the flavor. To thicken the sauce, add the flour.

Hazel Rumney's Spanish Spaghetti Sauce

Many years ago, when my husband was in the military, we lived for four years in Zaragoza, Spain. The first two years off base were in a tiny Spanish village called Garrapinillos. I got this recipe from a neighbor. I've tweaked it a bit because I don't like really spicy food. I don't put in the hot sausage, and I use garlic powder instead of garlic salt. Sometimes I still add pepperoni in the last half hour, if I have it on hand. It's been over thirty years, and I still use this recipe.

Add the beef, onion, and green pepper to a stockpot and cook at medium-high until the meat is done and the onions and peppers are soft. Drain.

Add the tomato paste, tomatoes with liquid, oregano, chili powder, garlic powder, salt, and pepper. Cover the pot and simmer for 30 to 45 minutes.

Add the apple cider vinegar and brown sugar. Cover the pot and simmer 30 minutes more.

1 pound ground beef or hot sausage
1 small onion, chopped
1 medium green pepper
1 (12-ounce) can tomato paste
1 (24-ounce) can tomatoes, whole with liquid
1 teaspoon oregano
2 teaspoons chili powder
1 teaspoon garlic powder or a clove of garlic
Salt, to taste
Pepper, to taste
1 teaspoon apple cider vinegar
2 teaspoons brown sugar

Nicole Maddalo's Great-Grandma Annunziata's Italian Sauce

MAKES ENOUGH SAUCE FOR TWO 1-POUND BOXES OF SPAGHETTI

When I was growing up, my mother used to make this original Italian sauce for us. Her own mother, my grandmother, had learned how to make it from my great-grandmother, Annunziata Caruso, who hailed from Naples, Italy. Annunziata had taught my grandmother to make this sauce so that she'd be able to feed her son, my grandfather, properly when serving spaghetti. When I got married, my mother taught me how to make it. Now my husband begs me to make this sauce, and the recipe is so delicious that I am always asked how it's done, but of course I've left that a fair secret—until now. Enjoy!

1 (24-ounce) can crushed tomatoes
1 (12-ounce) can tomato paste
Water, enough to fill the tomato paste can
    2½ times
1 whole bay leaf
¼ teaspoon chopped basil
2½ teaspoons minced garlic
1 tablespoon garlic powder
1 tablespoon dried oregano (or more, if desired)
1 teaspoon Italian seasoning (or more,
    if desired)
¼ cup Parmesan cheese grated (or more,
    if desired)
¼ cup dried parsley flakes
¼ cup finely chopped onion
¼ teaspoon salt, or to taste
¼ teaspoon pepper, or to taste
Pinch of sugar (to reduce the acidity of the
    tomato sauce)
Meatballs, pork, or sausage (preferably sweet
    sausage), singly or in combination, to add
    flavor

In a large Crock-Pot/slow cooker, or a regular large pot, pour in the crushed tomatoes. Add to the pot the tomato paste and water. Add the bay leaf (which you will remove after the sauce is cooked) and the rest of the ingredients, except the meat. Be sure to brown the meat, then add it to the sauce. Allow the sauce to simmer for 2 hours at low heat. Taste and add ingredients, if desired.

Note: If you use a Crock-Pot/slow cooker, you will not have to stir. If you use a regular large cooking pot, stir frequently.

Sharon Magee's Thick and Meaty Sauce

MAKES 25 OR MORE SERVINGS

I've always disliked spaghetti sauce so watery it ran on the plate. So I set out to make a sauce that wouldn't run, thus the reason behind this thick and chunky spaghetti sauce, with its diced tomatoes squeezed dry. And being a carnivore at heart, I wanted a lot of meat. This recipe is the result of those efforts. It's become an often-requested family favorite and stars at our family's traditional spaghetti dinner the night before Thanksgiving. It stars also when we have guests. Or just because. This recipe makes a large amount, but it freezes well. We often send sauce-filled containers home with family and friends.

Heat the olive oil in a large skillet over medium-high heat. Stir in the Italian seasoning and salt, then add the mushrooms, onions, and garlic. Sauté until the onions are transparent and the mushrooms are softened.

Add the sausage links and ground beef. Cook the meat/onion mixture, stirring occasionally, until the meat is well browned, with no pink remaining. Drain well.

As the meat/onion mixture is browning, put the drained diced tomatoes in a piece of cheesecloth and ring from them the remaining liquid. They should be as juice-free as possible, with only the pulp remaining.

Transfer the meat/onion mixture to a large pot over low heat. Add the spaghetti sauce, diced tomatoes, tomato paste, and black olives.

Cook on low heat for several hours, stirring occasionally. The longer the sauce cooks, the more the flavors meld. Adjust the spices as needed. This is great as spaghetti sauce or for dipping with bread.

¼ cup olive oil

2 tablespoons Italian seasoning

1 teaspoon salt

1 (16-ounce) can mushrooms, sliced

1 large yellow onion, peeled and chopped

1 tablespoon garlic, minced

1 (1-pound, 3-ounce) package sweet sausage links, casings removed and cut into bite-size pieces

1 (1-pound, 3-ounce) package hot or spicy sausage links, casings removed and cut into bite-size pieces

1 pound ground beef

5 (14.5-ounce) cans diced Italian-flavored tomatoes, drained

5 (24-ounce) bottles thick and chunky spaghetti sauce

1 (12-ounce) can tomato paste

2 (3.8-ounce) cans sliced black olives, drained

Rocky Gibbons's To-Die-For Ham Dipping Sauce

MAKES ABOUT 2 CUPS

I love rich sauces (and don't my hips show it!). This mustard cream dipping sauce is great on ham and other meats as well. Once you try it, you'll never have ham again without it!

½ cup sugar
1 tablespoon dry mustard, or more to taste
3 tablespoons flour
1 egg, beaten
½ cup vinegar
1 cup whipping cream

Mix all the ingredients and simmer over water in a double boiler (you don't want to burn it). Stir the sauce until it thickens, then take it off the heat, and it's done.

"I love cooking with wine - sometimes I even put it in the food."

—Julia Child, W.C. Fields, Rocky Gibbons, Sherry Monahan, and who-knows-who-else-has-used-this-quote!

Candy Moulton's Chokecherry Syrup

MAKES 1–3 CUPS, DEPENDING UPON YOUR BERRY CROP

Begin this recipe by making the juice and then the syrup. You cannot count on a new batch of chokecherry syrup every year because sometimes the weather does not cooperate and there are not many cherries; other years the birds beat you to them! One of my favorite things about chokecherry syrup is the smell that fills the house when the cherries are cooking. As far as the proportions, well . . . I use a bucket anywhere from the size of a coffee can to 5 gallons—depending on how good the berries are during the year. So I might have 3 cups of juice or maybe a couple gallons of juice. The key is to mix juice and sugar in the proportions in the recipe.

I suppose a 1-gallon ice cream bucket or 3-pound coffee can might yield about 3 or 4 cups of juice. And 3 cups of juice will yield 2 or 3 pints of syrup. Honestly . . . I don't keep track of that stuff. I just mix whatever juice I have with sugar in proper proportion and then put it in the hot jars and seal them. Whatever is left over goes in the syrup pitcher for pancakes the next day, or maybe for supper.

For the juice: Pick a bucket of chokecherries (they grow wild along streams in the West and ripen in mid to late August). Wash them to remove any leaves (it is OK to leave the stems on, though I usually don't). Put the chokecherries in a big pot of water and boil. Drain and hold the juice in a separate container. You can add more water and boil a second time to get more juice, if desired.

Throw the spent berries out for the birds because they love chokecherries. I suppose if you live in a city, you might want to put them in a mulch bed.

For the syrup: To make the syrup, start with a large pot. Mix 3 cups of chokecherry juice with 2½ cups of sugar. Boil this hard for 5 minutes, or until it is slightly thickened. Pour the hot syrup into clean, hot mason jars. Seal the jars with new lids.

Note: The syrup when at full boil will fill a large pot, and when I first started making this syrup, I always boiled it over and made a big mess on the stove. Then my mom and Aunt Jeanette told me the simple trick of dropping in a half-teaspoon of butter when it's at full boil. This will settle the syrup and eliminate cleanup challenges!

3 cups chokecherry juice
Water
2½ cups sugar

Krista Soukup's Grandmother's Chocolate Sauce

SERVES 6

My kids and I love ice cream and enjoy making this special sauce together. This is an old family recipe of my Grandma Olive's, of whom I have so many special memories helping her in the kitchen and eating her delicious homemade food. I think of her every time we make this sauce, which makes it extra sweet. She was a lovely and caring grandma who baked and cooked for anyone visiting her home on a Minnesota lake, where the record player turned cowboy tunes and my grandpa sang along and danced. My grandparents' favorite places were "out West," where they traveled to their entire lives.

¼ cup sugar
3 tablespoons cocoa
1 tablespoon cornstarch
1 cup water
2 tablespoons butter
1 teaspoon vanilla

Combine the sugar, cocoa, cornstarch, and water in a medium saucepan. Bring to a boil over high heat and boil 1 minute.

Remove from the heat and add the butter and vanilla. Stir to combine. Serve warm over ice cream.

Susan D. Matley's Wally's (Her Horse) Oat Cakes

MAKES 9 OR 10 OAT CAKES

My friend Wally, the (mostly) quarter horse and paint that ain't, gets a batch of these in his Christmas stocking every year. He enjoys this original recipe, created especially for him. From what I've read, the ingredients are wholesome for horses, but feel free to do your own checking.

Thoroughly combine all the ingredients in a medium-size mixing bowl and let the mixture sit at room temperature for 1 hour.

Heat the oven to 350°F. Coat a cookie sheet with cooking spray.

By rounded tablespoon, drop the mixture onto the cookie sheet and gently flatten the drops. Place the cookie sheet in the oven, reduce the heat to 300°F, and bake the cakes for 20 minutes or until they feel firm to the touch. Remove the oat cakes to a rack to cool.

¾ cup rolled oats
⅔ cup frozen corn kernels, thawed
¼ cup cornmeal
¼ cup wheat flour
½ cup grated carrot
¼ cup milk
¼ cup unsweetened applesauce
1 tablespoon molasses

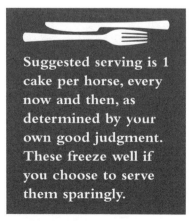

Suggested serving is 1 cake per horse, every now and then, as determined by your own good judgment. These freeze well if you choose to serve them sparingly.

ABOUT THE CONTRIBUTORS

T. Lindsay Baker is the author of two dozen books on the history of the American West, and is known to many Western Writers of America members as the man who spent a year and a half living in a dirt-floored sod house on the southern Great Plains in the Texas Panhandle. He holds the W. K. Gordon Endowed Chair in Texas Industrial History at Tarleton State University; he and his wife, Julie, live on his great-grandparents' farm between Fort Worth and Waco, Texas.

Christy and Selah Award winner and finalist author **Stephen Bly** authored and coauthored with his wife, Janet, more than 105 fiction and nonfiction books, including historical and contemporary Westerns. He mentored hundreds of beginning writers; spoke for writer's conferences, men's retreats, and family camps across the country; and as an avid collector of antique Winchesters and gun show participant, was roving editor for *Big Show Journal*. He served as mayor of Winchester, Idaho, and also pastored churches in California and Idaho. For more information, go to www.BlyBooks.com.

Johnny D. Boggs is a past president of Western Writers of America and six-time Spur Award winner. He lives in Santa Fe, New Mexico, where he edits WWA's *Roundup™* magazine. A South Carolina native, Boggs worked fourteen and half years in Texas as a newspaper journalist in Dallas and Fort Worth before moving to New Mexico in 1998 to write books and magazine articles full-time. Other honors include a Western Heritage Wrangler Award, the New Mexico Department of Agriculture's Rounders Award, and a Distinguished Alumnus Award from the University of South Carolina School of Journalism and Mass Communications. His website is www.Johnny DBoggs.com.

Natalie Bright is an author, blogger, speaker, and cattle ranch owner. Her stories and articles have appeared in numerous publications, including "A Cowboy's Christmas Blessing" in *West Texas Christmas Stories* by TCU Press. She holds a BBA from WTSU, enjoys talking to all ages about writing, and is dedicated to promoting a better understanding of the Western lifestyle. Follow her on Facebook, Twitter @natNKB, Amazon Author Pages, Instagram, or LinkedIn. Her website is nataliebright.com. She blogs every Monday about story craft at wordsmithsix.com.

Historian and author **Nancy Burgess** is a Phoenix native and has a lifelong interest in and passion for Arizona history. *Ranch Dog*, a tribute to the working dog in the American West, was published in 2000. *A Photographic Tour of 1916 Prescott, Arizona* was published in 2005 and reprinted in 2015. In 2012 Nancy completed two books, *Around Yavapai County, Celebrating Arizona's Centennial* and *An Illustrated History of Mayer, Arizona: Stagecoaches, Mining, Ranching and the Railroad. An Arizona Auto Adventure: Clarence Boynton's 1913 Travelogue* was published in 2013. Nancy is a dedicated, longtime collector of Arizona postcards and photographs, and her books have been extensively illustrated with images from her collections. She was honored as an Arizona Culturekeeper in 2008 and received the Sharlot Hall Award in 2010 and the Prescott Western Heritage Foundation Award in 2013.

Award-winning author, historian, and lecturer **Jan Cleere** writes extensively about the people who first settled in the desert Southwest. She is the author of five historical nonfiction books and featured in three anthologies. Jan is a Road Scholar with the Arizona Humanities Council, serves on the Coordinating Council of the Arizona Women's Heritage Trail, and is a board member of the Arizona Authors Association. She also writes a monthly column for Tucson's *Arizona Daily Star*, Western Women, detailing the lives of some of Arizona's early amazing women.

Nancy Coggeshall has been a freelance writer in Rhode Island, New Mexico, and rural Quebec. Her first book, *Gila Country Legend: The Life and Times of Quentin Hulse*, bracketed by the account of her life with him, was published in 2009 and is now in paper. Quentin began cooking for cowboys at the age of twelve. He relished someone else cooking for him but stepped up for the tried-and-true New Mexico cowboy favorites: beans; red chile; menudo, a soup made with tripe; and another soup, posole, made with hominy and pork—though Quentin used pigs' feet.

Award-winning author **Paul Colt** favors unexpected history. His stories often feature some little-known or overlooked aspect of an otherwise familiar character or event. Paul's analytical insight, investigative research, and genuine horse sense bring history to life. His characters walk off the pages of history into the reader's imagination in a style that blends Jeff Shaara's historical dramatizations with Robert B. Parker's gritty dialogue.

Paul's first book with Five Star, *Boots and Saddles: A Call to Glory*, received the Marilyn Brown Novel Award, presented by Utah Valley University for excellence in unpublished work prior to its release in 2013. His *Grasshoppers in Summer* received finalist recognition in the Western Writers of America 2009 Spur Awards.

Paul's work in Western fiction gives creative expression to a lifelong love of the West. He gets his boots dirty researching a story, whenever possible from the back of a horse. Learn more at www.paulcolt.com.

Hank Corless is an American historian and freelance writer. His primary works in Western Americana consist of numerous short stories in Western journals such as *Old West* and *True West*, and he is the author of a nonfiction cultural work on Native Americans, *The Weiser Indians*, along with several genealogies. He serves on the writing staff of a sports organization, where his most recent literary endeavors include a great many articles on college sports and sports personalities. When not writing, Hank spends much of his time as a lecturer, tour guide, and exhibit host at the Idaho State Historical Society's Old Idaho Penitentiary site.

Carol Crigger got her first cookbook as an eight-year-old. She found the recipes tasted bland and were too simple, which probably led to her life-long penchant for tweaking recipes. Her strictest critic was not her brother, but an aunt known to visit at dinnertime. Upon being invited to eat, Aunt Effie would reply, "I couldn't eat a bite" or a terse "I've et." It depended on the menu. Carol learned the term *chiffonade* from TV cooking shows, although she's used the technique. Mostly, like her fictional heroine, China Bohannon, she is a bare-bones cook.

Kellen Cutsforth is the author of *Buffalo Bill, Boozers, Brothels, and Bare Knuckle Brawlers: An Englishman's Journal of Adventure in America*. He has also published numerous articles in *Wild West* magazine and Western Writers of America's *Roundup* magazine. Kellen has also provided his services as a professional "ghost writer," authoring biographies and memoirs. Along with those accomplishments, he is a longtime member and social media manager for WWA and the Western history group Denver Posse of Westerners. He is also a past president of the Denver Posse of Westerners.

Sandra Dallas is the *New York Times* best-selling author of fourteen novels, two young adult novels, and ten nonfiction books, almost all of them about the West. She is a three-time winner of the Western Writers of America Spur Award, for *The Chili Queen*, *Tallgrass*, and *The Last Midwife*, and a four-time winner of the Women Writing the West WILLA Award. In addition, she is the recipient of the Denver Public Library's Eleanor Gehres Award and the Pikes Peak Library District's Frank Waters Award. Sandra was Denver chief for *Business Week* magazine and the publication's first female bureau manager.

First published in her teens by a men's magazine, **Barbara Dan** continued writing in a variety of genres before accepting a dare from her brother, poet Alan MacDougall, in 1988 to write a "bodice ripper." Since then she has written twelve historical romance novels, including five Westerns. Her latest, *Home Is Where the Heart Is*, features a resourceful young lady, Meg, who boards an orphan train to get to her new job on a Wyoming ranch. En route most orphans get adopted, except three. When Sam, her employer, finds himself saddled with a ready-made family, all hell breaks out!

Terry Del Bene is an archaeologist and has authored several books, including the *Donner Party Cookbook*, *Phone on the Range*, and *'Dem Bon'z*, among others. He writes freelance articles about the West for various publications and has a monthly series in *True West* magazine titled *Survival Out West*. You can learn the history they never taught you in school at www.pulphistory.com.

Robert Flynn is the author of ten novels. *Wanderer Springs* and *Echoes of Glory* received Spur Awards; *North to Yesterday* received a Wrangler Award from the National Cowboy Hall of Fame. He has also written two memoirs and three short story collections. His latest book is *Holy Literary License: The Almighty Chooses Fallible Mortals to Write, Edit and Translate GodStory*.

Nicole Maddalo Dixon was born in Philadelphia but moved to Bucks County, Pennsylvania, with her family at the age of thirteen, where she still resides with her husband, Wallace. She has been writing since the age of six. She finally decided to compose a series worth publication in 2009, and in 2012 she submitted the manuscript for the first book in her series, *Bandita Bonita: Romancing Billy the Kid*, and was excited to have been accepted. The second book in the series, *Bandita Bonita and Billy the Kid: The Scourge of New Mexico*, was released in 2016. Her website is www.nicolemdixonauthor.com.

Emil Franzi was born in Boston and raised in Glendale, California. His father was in the theater business and as a kid, he saw many Westerns and "later got cute girls jobs selling candy." A member of Phi Kappa Psi, he graduated from the University of Arizona in the 1960s with a BA in history. He had various endeavors from copy writer to political consultant, and is a lifer Young Republican. Franzi has been a newspaper and magazine columnist, did freelance work, and added radio host to his list of careers in the '90s. His wife, Kathleen, had real job and paid the mortgage. They've lived on twenty acres in the Tortolitas, which is northwest of Tucson, since 1973. He and his wife have been married for fifty-one years. They have three daughters, one granddaughter, and four dogs. Franzi started the radio program *Voices of the West* in 2006 and it is currently heard as a Podcast. In 2014 he was awarded Western Writers of America's Lariat Award.

Micki Fuhrman grew up in a river town in northwest Louisiana, where stories hung in the air at church picnics, back porch singings, and country store counters. She first wrote poetry for a school newspaper and by her teens was a professional singer/songwriter, appearing on the *Louisiana Hayride* and guest-starring on the *Grand Ole Opry*. Now a Nashville resident, Micki segued into literary writing in 2013. She has won awards for her short fiction (2015 WWA Spur Finalist, 2015 Western Fictioneers Peacemaker Finalist) and is at work on a novel set in the Cherokee Territory of Appalachia. She loves driving back roads, antiquing, and cooking for crowds.

Rachelle "Rocky" Gibbons grew up along the San Pedro River in southern Arizona. Her writing career began in 1975, when she wrote advertising copy for Columbia Pictures radio station KCPX in Salt Lake City. She then went on to become a broadcast media buyer for Western International Media of Los Angeles. The Big Buckaroo character in her children's books is based on her late cousin, rodeo star and Robbers Roost rancher A. C. Ekker. She is presently working on a juvenile fiction book and a biography of Bridget Sullivan, the Irish maid from the infamous Lizzie Borden trial. Rocky lives in the peaceful community of Central, Utah, with her husband and dogs.

Bill Groneman was born and raised in New York City and now lives in Texas. He writes about John Steinbeck, Davy Crockett, the Alamo, and September 11, 2001. Bill has been a member of the Western Writers of America since 1993 and has served on the WWA's executive board twice. He looks forward to attending the WWA's convention every year, where he lends his voice and guitar to the nightly music. He is the composer of the song *Western Writers of America* and founder of the fabulous "Gronettes" chorus line.

USA Today best-selling author **Shanna Hatfield** writes character-driven romances with relatable heroes and heroines. Her historical Westerns have been described as "reminiscent of the era captured by *Bonanza* and *The Virginian*," while her contemporary works have been called "laugh-out-loud funny, and a little heart-pumping sexy without being explicit in any way."

Convinced everyone deserves a happy ending, this hopeless romantic is out to make it happen, one story at a time. When she isn't writing or indulging in chocolate (dark and decadent, please), Shanna hangs out with her husband, lovingly known as Captain Cavedweller.

Jan C. Hill was born and raised on Long Island, New York. As a child she loved watching TV Westerns so much that she was known as "Texanna Wells" to her playground friends! A graduate of both Marymount College and Hofstra University, she taught children with special needs for over thirty years. Now retired, Jan has more time to accompany her author husband Bill on their many trips along the Western trails. She coauthored their activity books for young children, *Heading West, Heading Southwest, This Is the Place, West with Lewis and Clark,* and *Riding with the Pony.*

Anne Hillerman is the author of the continuation of the popular Joe Leaphorn/Jim Chee mysteries series created by her father, Tony Hillerman, and updated to include a powerful woman crime-solver, Bernadette Manuelito. Anne began her writing career as a newspaper reporter, and continues in journalism with the juicy job of restaurant critic for the *Albuquerque Journal*. She learned to cook from her mother, beginning with grilled cheese sandwiches, and considers home-cooked meals worth the effort—at least most days. A New Mexican since the age of four, she lives in Santa Fe with her husband, photographer Don Strel. She's also a Spur winner.

Award-winning author **Tammy Hinton** explains, "I don't want to live anywhere where men don't wear boots and a Stetson hat." Maybe that has an influence on her desire to write books that have a Western flavor. Her books *Unbridled* and *Retribution* won the prestigious Will Rogers Medallion Award and Best Western Novel from the Western Fictioneers. *Unbridled* also was a finalist for the Spur Award from Western Writers of America and the WILLA Award from Women Writing the West.

Ms. Hinton earned a BS in education from Black Hills State University. While there, Friends of the Leland D. Case Library for Western Historical Studies presented her a scholarship for her academic achievement. Visit http://www.tammyhinton.com

Denzel Holmes started writing after a thirty-one-year career as an auditor with the federal government. He is a product of rural West Texas, where he was regaled with cowboy and Indian tales from early youth. Western was a natural genre when he acted on his lifelong desire to write at age fifty-seven. When he joined Western Writers of America, he lowered the average member age by ten years. Published by Trebleheart Books from 2009 to 2012, when Lee Emory closed out her business, he self-published and continued to use the same editor. He has six novels now.

Her parents were always seeking greener grass, so **Maxine Isackson** was often the new kid in school. She found new friends in books. With her love of books, it was only natural she began writing when her own children were grown. She did a lot of freelance articles then turned to Western fiction, taking material from the old-timers she admired. She has published eight books and has another in the chute. Her website is maxine isackson.com.

Linda Jacobs is the author of the WILLA and Spur award–winning Yellowstone Series of novels—*Summer of Fire, Rain of Fire, Lake of Fire,* and *Jackson Hole Journey*—and two contemporary romances. Linda also had a thirty-year career as a professional petroleum geologist in Houston. Now retired to her family farm in Virginia, she and her husband, Richard, love adventure travel and reading the next great Western.

Born on the Klamath Reservation in Oregon and enrolled with the Modoc tribe of Oklahoma, **Cheewa James** has authored *MODOC: The Tribe That Wouldn't Die* and three other books on Native people. She has written for *True West, Smithsonian, National Wildlife,* and newspapers across the country. A former TV anchorwoman and reporter, Cheewa feels learning to write in short sentences, right to the point, and using expressive, simple words was a great guide as she developed her writing. Currently a professional motivational speaker, she says, "Being a good storyteller is important both on the platform and in creating a story on paper."

Gail L. Jenner and her fourth-generation-cowboy husband live on the 140-year-old family homestead. Gail and six other "Jenner women" have created Jenner Family Beef, selling 100 percent all-natural, ranch-bred beef locally and online. Today Jenner Cattle Company continues its historic traditions, including processing its own beef, hams, bacon, sausages, even apple cider! A teacher, Gail has written ten books, including seven nonfiction titles and the WILLA Award–winning *Across the Sweet Grass Hills*. She is a California Cattle Woman, gardener, and award-winning cook with recipes appearing in *Better Homes & Gardens*, *Everyday with Rachael Ray*, and *Country Woman* magazines.

Singer/songwriter and author **Jim Jones** is a native Texan, a student of the West, and a lifelong devotee of all things cowboy. He is an award-winning musician and author, producing nine Western folk albums, three Western novels, and a compilation of his blog titled *Western Takes: Perspectives on the Meaning of Life and Other Stuff*. His fourth novel, *The Big Empty*, was published by Five Star in 2016. He lives in Albuquerque, New Mexico, with his wife, Ann, and their two dogs, Jessie and Colter.

Colorado author **Joyce B. Lohse** combines her journalism education and background, genealogy research skills, and a passion for history to preserve and share stories of Western pioneers through award-winning biographies, articles, and presentations. Subjects include Molly Brown, Baby Doe Tabor, General William Palmer, Dr. Justina Ford, educator Emily Griffith, and the original governor and first lady of Colorado, John and Eliza Routt. Her latest title is *Spencer Penrose: Builder and Benefactor*. Lohse has made appearances and presented programs at over 150 events during the past decade. She is longtime administrator for Women Writing the West. Her website is www.LohseWorks.com.

Sharon Magee, a Phoenix-based writer and award-winning author, specializes in history with a heavy emphasis on the American Indian. She is also a generalist with extensive publishing credits in such magazines as *Arizona Highways*, *Phoenix Magazine*, *The Valley Guide Quarterly*, *Priorities*, and *Phoenix Downtown*. Magee has won numerous awards, including the Outstanding Writing Award from the Arizona Newspaper Foundation. She also wrote the award-winning *Geronimo! Stories of an American Legend* and was a contributing author to *Arizona Goes to War*, also an award winner. She and her husband live in Phoenix. Between them they have four beautiful children and three awesome grandsons.

History has fascinated **Bill Markley** since childhood on the family farm near Valley Forge, Pennsylvania. Moving to Pierre, South Dakota, in 1976 to work for the state's Department of Environment and Natural Resources, he immersed himself in local history, leading to participating in films such as *Dances with Wolves*. Bill has written a novel, *Deadwood Dead Men*; three Western nonfiction books; and for *True West* and *Wild West* magazines. He has served for 25 years as Western Writers of America's membership chairman, writes *Roundup's*™ *Techno-Savvy*, and served on the board of directors. In 2015 Bill was sworn in as an honorary Dodge City Marshal. Bill and his wife, Liz, live in Pierre, where they have raised two grown children.

Susan Matley writes sci-fantasy and Western historical fiction. Her sci-fantasy novella *Small-g City* (by S. D. Matley) is her first published book-length work. Previously, her short stories have appeared in the THEMA literary journal, *GlassFire* magazine, and *Dark Pages* (Blade Red Press). She's a member of Western Writers of America and Women Writing the West. In 2011 she was a finalist for the WWA "Best Song" Spur Award. Susan lives near Walla Walla, Washington, amidst thousands of acres of wheat (not hers!) with husband Bruce and many four-legged kids.

Shoni Maulding twists horse tail hairs together to make hitched horsehair art. Her husband, Ron, adds silver and stones. For museum-quality pieces, they have a story—like their award-winning ensemble *Flight of the Nez Perce*. Or using Montana jasper on rosettes for their *Griz on Horse Prairie* bridle. Shoni received the Will Rogers Cowboy Award from the Academy of Western Artists and was inducted into the Stetson Craftsman Alliance. She has been a technical adviser for others on various projects and teaches hitching workshops. Ron and Shoni's how-to books have sold in twenty-three countries. They live on the Flathead Indian Reservation in Montana. Their website is www.hitchedhorsehair.com.

When not scaling mountain peaks or fording raging rivers, Team Gritty—award-winning photographer and videographer **Jennifer Smith-Mayo**, Spur Award–winning author **Matthew P. Mayo**, and Tess the Wonderpup—run Gritty Press (www.GrittyPress.com) and rove North America in search of hot coffee, tasty whiskey, and high adventure.

Monty McCord is a retired law enforcement officer and graduate of the FBI National Academy at Quantico, Virginia. He served as a deputy sheriff in two sheriff's offices before retiring from the Hastings, Nebraska, police department as a lieutenant. An avid interest in history, especially of lawmen, led to the writing life. He serves as president of the Adams County Historical Society board of directors and is a member of the Western Writers of America. McCord writes fiction and nonfiction about lawmen and outlaws from the Old West to the mid-twentieth century. In 2015 Monty was sworn in as an honorary Dodge City Marshal.

Dennis McCown is a college instructor in Texas. Born and raised in Wyoming, he is proud of his "cowboy" heritage. Though he has traveled widely, he always comes back to his roots. After hearing about Helen Mrose, McCown spent sixteen years researching her incredible story, which resulted in *The Goddess of War: A True Story of Passion, Betrayal, and Murder in the Old West.* Under the pseudonym Butch Denny, he published *Savage Winter: A Story of Wilderness and Survival.* A member of the Western Writers of America, McCown is also in the Wild West History Association and the Single-Action Shooting Society.

Sandra McGee has a fascination with the Reno divorce era of the 1930s and '40s that began three decades ago when she met her husband, Bill McGee, a former dude wrangler on Nevada's most exclusive dude ranch that catered to wealthy Easterners and Hollywood celebrities, most seeking a six-week divorce. Together they wrote about this little-known period of contemporary Western history in *The Divorce Seekers: A Photo Memoir of a Nevada Dude Wrangler* (print edition) and *The Cowboyin' Years, 1947–1950* (Kindle edition). When not writing, Sandra's passions are movies from the 1930s and '40s and ballet.

William L. McGee was born and raised on a ranch in Montana. After the war, from 1947 to 1950, he was a horse wrangler in Yellowstone National Park, a trail and deer-hunting guide at Lake Tahoe, and a dude wrangler on the Flying M.E., Nevada's most exclusive dude ranch outside of Reno that catered to wealthy Easterners and Hollywood celebrities, most seeking a six-week divorce. Bill and his coauthor/wife, Sandra, captured his stories in his memoir set in the contemporary West: *The Divorce Seekers: A Photo Memoir of a Nevada Dude Wrangler* (print) and *The Cowboyin' Years, 1947–1950* (Kindle).

Three-time winner and three-time finalist for the WWA Spur Award, **Rod Miller** writes fiction, history, and poetry about his lifelong home, the American West. A former member of the WWA executive board and longtime membership chair, Miller received the Branding Iron Award in 2014 for his service to Western Writers of America. His taste buds rattled loose during his years riding rodeo bucking horses, so his food preferences are plain and simple. He is not impressed with fancy "plating" or "presentation" and finds the word "foodie" unappetizing.

Tucson author **Susan Cummins Miller**, a research affiliate of the University of Arizona's Southwest Institute for Research on Women, worked as a field geologist and college instructor before turning to writing fiction, non-fiction, and poetry. She edited *A Sweet, Separate Intimacy: Women Writers of the American Frontier, 1800–1922*; pens the award-winning Frankie MacFarlane, Geologist mysteries; and publishes poems, short stories, and essays in regional journals and anthologies, including *What Wildness Is This: Women Write about the Southwest* and *Roundup! Western Writers of America Presents Great Stories of the West from Today's Leading Western Writers*. Her website is www.susancumminsmiller.com.

Award-winning author **Meg Mims** writes historical and contemporary novels, novellas, and short stories plus hundreds of freelance articles. She earned a Best First Novel Spur Award from Western Writers of America for *Double Crossing* and a Laramie Award for the sequel *Double or Nothing*. Meg is also one-half of the D. E. Ireland writing team for the Agatha-nominated Eliza Doolittle & Henry Higgins mystery series. She'll be writing as Meg Macy for a new cozy mystery series featuring a teddy bear toy shop for Kensington in 2017. A resident of southeastern Michigan, Meg enjoys gardening, crafts, watercolor painting, and housework last.

Sherry Monahan served as Western Writers of America's president from 2014 to 2016 and began her author career when she penned her first book, *Taste of Tombstone*, in 1998. It was her passion for food and history that led her to create that first book. She now has several books on daily life and women in the West. That same passion landed her a monthly magazine column in 2009 when she began writing her food column in *True West* titled *Frontier Fare*. Her last two books were historical cookbooks called *Frontier Fare* and *The Cowboy's Cookbook*. She's also written for *Arizona Highways* and *Cowboys & Indians*.

Sherry has appeared on Bill O'Reilly's *Legends and Lies*, AHC's *Gunslingers*, and on the History Channel in many shows. She earned a Wrangler in the 2010 Western Heritage Awards for her performance in the *Cowboys and Outlaws* show. In 2015 Sherry was sworn in as an honorary Dodge City Marshal. In 2016, she was awarded the Gold Will Rogers Medallion for *The Cowboy's Cookbook*. Her website is www.sherrymonahan.com.

David Morrell is the critically acclaimed author of *First Blood*, the novel in which Rambo was created. He holds a PhD in American literature from Penn State and was a professor in the English department at the University of Iowa. His numerous *New York Times* best-sellers include the classic spy novel, *The Brotherhood of the Rose* (the basis for the only television miniseries to be broadcast after a Super Bowl). An Edgar and Anthony finalist, and Nero and Macavity winner, Morrell is a recipient of three Bram Stoker Awards from the Horror Writers Association and the prestigious Thriller Master award from the International Thriller Writers organization. His writing book, *The Successful Novelist: A Lifetime of Lessons about Writing and Publishing*, discusses what he has learned in his more than four decades as an author. He lives in Santa Fe, New Mexico.

Wyoming native **Candy Moulton** has written thirteen Western history books; coedited a collection of short fiction and an encyclopedia; and written, produced, and been a reenactor in several documentary films. She won a Spur Award from Western Writers of America in 2006 for her biography, *Chief Joseph: Guardian of the People*. She won another Spur in 2010 for *In Pursuit of a Dream*, the documentary film she wrote and produced with Boston Productions Inc. (BPI) for the Oregon-California Trails Association. *Footsteps to the West* for the National Historic Trails Interpretive Center in Casper, Wyoming, was a Spur finalist for Best Documentary in 2003.

John Nesbitt lives in the plains country of Wyoming, where he teaches English and Spanish at Eastern Wyoming College. His articles, reviews, fiction, and poetry have appeared in numerous magazines and anthologies. He has had more than thirty books published, including short story collections, contemporary novels, and traditional Westerns, as well as textbooks for his courses. John has won two awards from the Wyoming State Historical Society, two awards from Wyoming Writers for encouragement of other writers and service to the organization, two Wyoming Arts Council literary fellowships, a Will Rogers Medallion Award for *Dark Prairie* and another for *Thorns on the Rose*, a Western Writers of America Spur finalist award for his novel *Raven Springs*, and the Spur Award for *At the End of the Orchard* and for his novels *Trouble at the Redstone* and *Stranger in Thunder Basin*. His most recent work consists of *Field Work*, a retro-noir fiction collection; *Thorns on the Rose*; and *Justice at Redwillow*.

Thom Nicholson was born in Missouri and raised around Fort Smith, Arkansas. He grew up watching local rodeos and admiring the bronc riders until he found out the hard way just how demanding that profession was. After an engineering degree, he joined the US Army and served as a Green Beret for thirty years, serving in Vietnam, South America, and Africa. In Vietnam he was a raider company commander for a cross-border operations unit. He retired from the army in the late nineties as a colonel and has been writing ever since.

Nicholson is a graduate of the National Defense University and instructed at the Command and General Staff School. He has his MBA from Pepperdine University and is a registered engineer and an enrolled agent for the IRS. He skis, scuba dives, and plays a fairly mean game of golf. He and his wife, Sandy, live in Colorado, close to the ski slopes and the grandkids.

Ann Noble received a BA in history and education from Bowdoin College in Brunswick, Maine, and an MA in history from the University of Utah. She has published several historical works, including books about Pinedale, the Heart Mountain Japanese American Relocation Center, a biography of W. N. "Neil" McMurry, and numerous articles about Wyoming, Western, and women's history.

Ms. Noble and her husband, David, own and operate a cattle ranch in Cora, Wyoming. They are the parents of four daughters who are the fifth generation on the ranch. Ms. Noble also is the owner of the historic Chambers House Bed and Breakfast in Pinedale.

Nancy Plain is Western Writers of America's vice president (2016–18) and writes nonfiction for the young-adult reader. Her books on Western and frontier topics include biographies of the cowboy artist Charlie Russell, the Nez Perce leader Chief Joseph, the photographer Solomon Butcher, and the artist/ornithologist John James Audubon. Recognition for Nancy's work includes four Spur Awards, a YALSA Finalist Award from the American Library Association, the Nebraska Book Award, the Will Rogers Medallion Award, a Booklist Editors' Choice citation, and the National Outdoor Book Award. She joined Western Writers of America in 2008.

Novelist, writer, and book critic **Clay Reynolds** is the author of twenty published volumes and more than one thousand other publications ranging from short fiction to published recipes. A Spur Award winner for Western short fiction, he was also nominated for a Pulitzer Prize in 1992 for his novel *Franklin's Crossing*. His most recent novel is *Vox Populi*. A cook, not a chef, Clay loves the creative outlet preparing food affords. "Second to having people read your work, nothing beats having people eat and enjoy what you've prepared," he says. He teaches writing and literature at the University of Texas at Dallas and lives in a small community, Lowry Crossing.

Lucia Robson wrote *Ride the Wind* while working as a public librarian in Maryland. It made the *New York Times* best-seller list in 1982, won a Western Writers of America Spur Award, and has been in print ever since. Her ninth book, *Last Train from Cuernavaca*, also was awarded a Spur. After nine historical novels, she wrote *Devilish*, a contemporary mystery with a supernatural twist. In 2016 she was inducted into the Western Writers Hall of Fame.

At one time, **Vicky Rose** considered attending chef school but realized she was more of a down-home, "put it on the supper table every night" type of cook, rather than a gourmet. Her writing has never been described as gravy, but she hopes it is just as nourishing to the soul as her food is to the stomach. All her heroines like to cook, and all her heroes like to eat. Bon appétit, or as they say in the Old West, "Come and git it!"

Hazel Rumney has worked in the publishing business for over thirty years, most of that as an editor. She has always loved books and reading and was the first in her family to have a library card. Her older brother gave her a Western to read when she was in her early teens. She has never stopped reading them, and Westerns have always been her favorite genre. Hazel attended Merced Community College in Merced, California, and started her publishing career at Thorndike Press in 1983. When she called her mother to tell her where she was working, her mother asked, "How much are you paying them to let you work there?" Along with Thorndike Press, she has also worked at Yankee Books, Cengage Learning, and Five Star Publishing.

A Montana ranch wife who works the calving barn in the wee hours of winter and the hay fields driving tractor in summer, **Quackgrass Sally** loves to write about the West, when she's not out living it. She's hitched her covered wagon and ridden her Pony Express horse over thousands of miles of historic Western trails. You'll find her name on several Western film productions and museum interactive exhibits. A lifetime member of the National Pony Express Association, she's even carried the Olympic Torch via horseback. Currently WWA Spur Awards Chair, Quackgrass believes that "every gal can be a legend in her own time . . . with a good horse!"

Michael N. Searles, known as **Cowboy Mike**, has spent his life in the field of education. He has taught at the middle school, high school, and university levels, always with the hope of broadening understanding and influencing lives. His love affair with the West has been motivated by the realization of two major factors: the importance of the West in shaping the American character, and the role of African Americans and other minorities in that formation. He, as a historian, accepts the challenge and mandate to pass on lessons learned in our great national Corps of American Discovery.

Dawn Senior-Trask grew up in the log cabin her family built in the foothills of Wyoming's Snowy Range. No electricity or running water, and her mom cooked on a wood range and kept perishables in a cooler shaded by the bushy juniper outside their door. Meals have never tasted better! Her father was a published author, her sister and brother wrote poems and songs, and her mom wrote down the poems Dawn made up and told to her since age four. Now she's working on a childhood memoir and cooking old recipes for her family!

Candace Simar is a Minnesota writer and poet. She has written the Spur Award–winning Abercrombie Trail Series, historical fiction about the Great Sioux Uprising of 1862. She also wrote *Farm Girls* and *Shelterbelts*. For more information, visit her website at www.candacesimar.com.

Brad Smith has been a member of the Western Writers of America since 2001. He has written twelve books about Arizona history and is a teacher at Cochise Elementary School. Brad and his wife, Audrey, reside in Cochise, Arizona.

Cotton Smith was born in Kansas City, Missouri; some would say a century later than he should have. He grew up enjoying both adjoining states, Kansas and Missouri, living mostly in Kansas. His ancestors fought in the Civil War, mostly for the South, as regulars and guerillas.

A gifted writer and thorough researcher, Cotton's extensive communications skills were widely evident early in life, as was his interest in the West. A past president of the Western Writers of America, Cotton's books garnered a Spur Award and the WWA Branding Iron Award. He has published twenty-one Western novels and cowrote three Western story anthologies. He is also the author of *Trail to Eagle*, a history of the early decades of Boy Scouting in Kansas City, and *Tribesmen Arise!*, the history of the Tribe of Mic-O-Say.

Krista Rolfzen Soukup is a literary publicist with over twenty-five years of experience in book promotion, marketing, and sales. As founder and owner of Blue Cottage Agency, she provides creative strategies and brand development for both new and experienced authors, as well as personalized guidance during every stage of book production, from prepublication through sales, advertising, and awards competitions. Through Blue Cottage Agency, Krista also promotes the literary arts as a whole, offering individuals and publishing companies a range of services that includes Web design and strategies for social media, publicity, and marketing. Krista speaks at regional and national writing conferences and participates in publishing and editing workshops. She also writes grants and organizes literary arts programs. In addition to holding a bachelor of science degree in business administration and marketing, Krista is a photographer who has been exhibited and published nationwide. She has been a member of Western Writers of America since 2013.

JoJo Thoreau started formulating stories when she was seven and published her first book, *Bendy Wendy* (2014), at age nine. She lives in a rural part of Maine and loves to visit schools to speak to other children about the magical world of reading and writing. When spending time at home, JoJo enjoys cuddling with her feline sidekicks, Boots and Trigger. Her second book, *Buckaroo Bobbie Sue* (2015), was awarded the WWA Spur Award. She's a member of Western Writers of America, Women Writing the West, and Maine Writers & Publishers Alliance. Learn more by visiting littlehandspress.org.

Susan Union is the author of the Randi Sterling Mystery Series. Her first book, *Rode to Death*, is set on a Southern California quarter horse breeding ranch and is available in paperback and in e-book format on Amazon, Nook, Kobo, and iBooks. The second in the series, *Paws for Death*, is also available in all e-book formats. Susan lives in Southern California with her family, her quarter horse mare, and her rescue dog, an Australian shepherd. To learn more about Susan, visit www.susanunion.com.

Neil Wetherington, or **Montana Kid Hammer**, a native Montanan, author, and educator, now resides in Fairbanks, Alaska. He enjoys a plethora of activities like shooting sports, American Civil War living history, and biblical studies. Retired military, Neil was educated at Hillsdale College and the Institute of Children's Literature. His series, *The Old West Adventures of Ornery and Slim*, is published by Authorhouse Publishing. Neil is an NRA Certified Instructor and holds life memberships with the National Rifle Association, the Single Action Shooting Society, and the Golden Heart Shootist Society, and is a colonel in the Honorable Order of Kentucky Colonels.

Sandy Whiting resides along a Kansas section of the Chisholm Trail. Although no cattle currently tread outside the door, an occasional horse and rider will trek up the paved street, and there are buffalo grazing in a pen about a mile and a half away. Sandy's first work of fiction appeared in *Louis L'Amour Western Magazine*. That story won the Spur Award for best short fiction. She has published several fiction stories as well as nonfiction articles.

G. R. Williamson is a historian, a Western writer, and a born storyteller. His publishing background includes three nonfiction books on the West, many magazine and newspaper articles, and several Western movie screenplays. Williamson's new novel, *T-Head Dead*, is a crime novel set in present-day Corpus Christi. As a member of the Western Writers of America, he's been on panel discussions discussing frontier gambling. He has appeared in a television documentary on famous feuds in the Old West. Williamson's home is in Kerrville, Texas, where he lives with his wife and Chihuahua, Shooter.

Author **R. G. Yoho** was born in Parkersburg, West Virginia, and grew up on a cattle farm in southeastern Ohio. His love of Westerns began with the reading of *Flint*, a novel by famed Western author Louis L'Amour.

Along with his five traditional Westerns, R. G. recently published his first work of historical fiction, *Return to Matewan*, which takes place during the coal mine wars in West Virginia and Colorado in the early twentieth century. A loving husband, father, and grandfather, Yoho has been married to his wife, JoEllen, for almost thirty-five years.

Michael Zimmer is the author of seventeen novels. His work has been praised by *Library Journal*, *Booklist*, *Publishers Weekly*, *Historical Novel Society*, and others. *City of Rocks* (Five Star, 2012) was chosen by Booklist as a top 10 Western novel for 2012. *The Poacher's Daughter* (Five Star, 2014) received a starred Booklist review and was awarded the National Cowboy & Western Heritage Museum's prestigious Western Heritage Wrangler Award for Outstanding Western Novel (2015). He is a two-time finalist for the Spur Award from the Western Writers of America and author of the *American Legends Collection* series. Zimmer resides in Utah with his wife, Vanessa, and their two dogs. Learn more by visiting his website at www.michael-zimmer.com.

CREDITS

Recipe Credits
Page 27 Courtesy of Trish Schmelzer
Pages 29, 94 Courtesy of Ann McCord
Page 46 Courtesy of Audrey Smith
Page 120 Courtesy of Melissa Elsmo
Pages 145, 146 Courtesy of Janet Chester Bly

Photo Credits
Page vi Photo File Name: 4a09143u, Credit: Library of Congress
Pages 1, 15, 47, 84, 129, 164 Photos by Sherry Monahan
Page 186 Photo courtesy of Tarleton State University, from the collection of T. Lindsey Baker
Page 186 Ridinger's Photography of Lewiston, Idaho, courtesy of Janet Chester Bly
Page 186 Photo by Johnny D. Boggs
Page 187 Photo by Lacy Johnston Photography from the collection of Natalie Bright
Page 187 Photo from the collection of Nancy Burgess
Page 187 Photo from the collection of Jan Cleere
Page 188 Photo from the collection of Nancy Coggeshall
Page 188 From the collection of Paul Colt
Page 188 From the collection of Hank Corless
Page 189 From the collection of Carol Crigger
Page 189 From the collection of Kellen Cutsforth
Page 189 Povy Kendal Atchison, from the collection of Sandra Dallas
Page 190 Photo from the collection of Barbara Dan
Page 190 Photo by Penelope Del Bene from the collection of Terry Del Bene
Page 190 Photo by Natalie Medina from the collection of Robert Flynn
Page 190 From the collection of Nicole Maddalo Dixon
Page 191 Photo of Emil Franzi by Sherry Monahan
Page 191 Photo from the collection of Micki Fuhrman
Page 191 Photo by Lynne Clark from the collection of Rachelle Gibbons
Page 192 From the collection of Bill Groneman

Page 192 Photos from the collection of Shanna Hatfield
Page 192 Photo by William B. Hill, from the collection of Jan C. Hill
Page 193 Photo by Jean Fogelberg from the Collection of Anne Hillerman
Page 193 Courtesy of Tammy Hinton
Page 193 From the collection of Denzel Holmes
Page 194 From the collection of Maxine Isackson
Page 194 Photo by Ollie Reed, Jr., from the collection of Linda Jacobs
Page 194 Photo by Allen Snyder, from the collection of Cheewa James
Page 195 Photos from the collection of Gail L. Jenner
Page 195 Photo by Lori Faith, photographybyfaith.com, from the collection of Jim Jones
Page 195 Photo by Don Lohse, from the collection of Joyce Lohse
Page 196 Collection of Sharon Magee
Page 196 Photo from the collection of Bill Markley
Page 196 Photo from the collection of Susan Matley
Page 197 Photo by Ron Maulding, from the collection of Shoni Maulding.
Page 197 From the collection of Matthew P. Mayo and Jennifer Smith Mayo
Page 197 Photo courtesy of Ann McCord
Page 198 Photo from the collection of Dennis McCown
Page 198 From the collection of Sandra McGee
Page 198 From the collection of Bill McGee
Page 199 From the collection of Rod Miller
Page 199 Photo by Clark Lohr, from the collection of Susan Cummins Miller
Page 199 Photo from the collection of Meg Mims
Page 200 Photos by Larry Monahan, from the collection of Sherry Monahan
Page 200 Photo by Jennifer Esperanza from the collection of David Morrell
Page 200 Photos from the collection of Candy Moulton
Page 201 From the collection of John Nesbitt
Page 201 From the collection of Thom Nicholson
Page 202 Photos by Blushing Crow Studio, from the collection of Ann Noble
Page 202 Photo of Nancy Plain by Sherry Monahan
Page 202 Photos from the collection of Clay Reynolds
Page 203 Photo from the collection of Lucia Robson
Page 203 Photo from the collection of Vicky Rose
Page 203 From the collection of Hazel Rumney
Page 204 Photo from the collection of Quackgrass Sally

Page 204 From the collection of Dawn Senior-Trask
Page 205 Photo of Candace Simar courtesy Krista Soukup
Page 205 Photo by Audrey Smith from the collection of Brad Smith
Page 205 Photo of Cotton Smith by Johnny D. Boggs
Page 206 Photo by Jema Anderson, from the collection of Krista Soukup
Page 206 Photo of JoJo Thoreau by Tiffany Schofield, from the collection of JoJo Thoreau
Page 206 Photo by Erika Union, from the collection of Susan Union
Page 207 Photo by Mykaela D. Stuart, from the collection of Neil Wetherington
Page 207 Photo from the collection of Sandy Whiting
Page 207 Photos from the collection of Ron Williamson
Page 208 Photo by Logan Yoho, from the collection of Robert Yoho
Page 208 Photo from the collection of Michael Zimmer

INDEX

ABOUT THE EDITORS

Sherry Monahan served as Western Writers of America's president from 2014 to 2016 and began her author career when she penned her first book, *Taste of Tombstone*, in 1998. It was her passion for food and history that led her to create that first book. She now has several books on daily life and women in the West. That same passion landed her a monthly magazine column in 2009 when she began writing her food column in *True West* titled "Frontier Fare." Her last two books were historical cookbooks called *Frontier Fare* and *The Cowboy's Cookbook*. She's also written for *Arizona Highways* and *Cowboys & Indians*.

Sherry has appeared on Bill O'Reilly's *Legends and Lies*, AHC's *Gunslingers*, and on the History Channel in many shows. She earned a Wrangler in the 2010 Western Heritage Awards for her performance in the *Cowboys and Outlaws* show. In 2015 Sherry was sworn in as an honorary Dodge City Marshal. Sherry was also awarded the Gold Will Rogers Medallion for *The Cowboy's Cookbook* in 2016. Her website is www.sherrymonahan.com.

Nancy Plain is Western Writers of America's vice president (2016–18) and writes nonfiction for the young-adult reader. Her books on Western and frontier topics include biographies of the cowboy artist Charlie Russell, the Nez Perce leader Chief Joseph, the photographer Solomon Butcher, and the artist/ornithologist John James Audubon. Recognition for Nancy's work includes four Spur Awards, a YALSA Finalist Award from the American Library Association, the Nebraska Book Award, the Will Rogers Medallion Award, a Booklist Editors' Choice citation, and the National Outdoor Book Award. She joined Western Writers of America in 2008.

Happy Cooking Trails from all of us at Western Writers of America!